To Exodus, and Beyond!

The Continuation of the Evaluation

By Steve Paull

Illustrated just as badly as before by
Steve Paull

Copyright © 2022 Steve Paull

ISBN: 978-1-922788-23-8
Published by Vivid Publishing
A division of Fontaine Publishing Group
P.O. Box 948, Fremantle
Western Australia 6959
www.vividpublishing.com.au

 A catalogue record for this
book is available from the
NATIONAL National Library of Australia
LIBRARY
OF AUSTRALIA

Dedicated to my son, who got pissed off with the first book being dedicated to Sue.

CONTENTS

Foreword

Hello dearest readers, and welcome to this, the second installment of our journey into the convoluted world of all things biblical. Those of you who have read (or better yet, actually purchased) my first volume will recall with varying degrees of fondness the time we had exploring the claims of Genesis, and what a wonderful time we had shoving a very large Crowbar of Modern Interpretation into the deepest nether regions of religious dogma. Religion, as we know well, is as prevalent in today's society as, say, the common cold. Indeed, with 4,200 religions of varying degrees of difference being worshipped in the world today, it's hard enough to decide if Religionism has any basis in fact at all, let alone which religion gets closest to the truth, whatever that may happen to be. It all depends on your own individual circumstances and prejudices, how you were brought up, what denomination you were brought up to believe in, your own considered thoughts on the subject, whatever "evidence" may be floating around to sway your position one way or the other, and a myriad other considerations.

But if you're here reading this book, I'm willing to bet that you're at the stage where you want a better excuse for why we're here than what is being offered by organized religion. You might be an atheist, or agnostic, or questioning, or just plain curious, and that's all perfectly fine by me. Even if you're religious (and obviously picked up this book by accident!), I would implore you to suspend your indoctrinated belief for a short time and explore the unlimited possibilities of existence with me; to question the dogma, to engage your mind in new and exciting ways, to dare to be skeptical. There's always the chance that you are super-religious with an unshakable faith, particularly in the face of the available evidence; and while that is your right as a human, I do feel sad for the way you have voluntarily restricted your intellectual horizons. It is my solemn hope that, whatever possessed you to grab this book, you will at least get as much of a chuckle out of it as the first book, and that perhaps you will find the odd epiphany that will set your imagination ablaze with those unlimited possibilities we were talking about earlier.

Life, as we know it, sucks. We are born, we live, we cry, we hurt, we work, we pay taxes, we procreate, we get old, and we die. That's pretty much it as far as our mortal coils are concerned. But what about that ineffable part of us that yearns to understand more about our universe? Not *how* we are here, as much as *why*? Is our consciousness merely the product of our biological processes, or is it more than the sum of our parts? Who knows, for an absolute certainty, our role in the grand scheme of things? I can tell you for an absolute certainty that it is NOT religion. Science gets close, but doesn't quite understand or embrace the metaphysical components that to this day elude the most sensitive of instruments, although they would very much like to one day. Nay, the only way to true enlightenment is to attempt to forge a logical middle path between Science and Superstition. We are often told that Truth is stranger than fiction, and whilst the bible can be arguably called the biggest work of fiction the world has ever known, these ideas had to originate from somewhere. Let's explore that together.

How to Read this Book

As with my last offering on this subject, my recommendation would be with an open mind, an active imagination, and an unhealthy sense of humour. Knowing how to read would be an added bonus, however if you're disadvantaged in that department, I suppose I could try to get Morgan Freeman to narrate the thing to you.

Well, perhaps not the remarkable Mr. Freeman, although how awesome would it be, right? No, for this particular subject matter, perhaps I would be better off asking the likes of Jim Jeffries to narrate it. The Australian accent would be accurate enough to make the humour work, at least. I'll have my people call his people and see what I can do for you, guys. No promises, though…

Volume Two (for this is certainly what it is) will be picking up pretty much where Volume One left off, and one of the largest assumptions I will make is that you've actually read Volume One and are ready to resume your odyssey with me into Exodus and beyond. If not, well that's okay. I'm sure you will get around to it eventually and enjoy it as much as I did when I wrote it. But for now, sit back and relax and we shall resume our journey.

The Story So Far

Here, then, is what we've covered thus far:

God considers and plans and ultimately creates the universe, without any means of existing prior to its creation, because nothing existed. He created earth and sea and plants, whales and lions and aardvarks and pangolins, then finally created Man in his own image, despite there being no frame of reference in regards to gender. He makes a garden paradise with one caveat, which Man (or more accurately, Woman) ignores completely, which gets them both booted out of paradise.

People then spring out of the ground everywhere with no explanation of where they might have been hiding. God's "angels" – his sons, staff or whatever - start getting busy with the daughters of Man and create Nephilim (the bible equivalent of medieval giants). Seeing his Divine Plan screwed about with every act of Free Will, he drowns everybody except an animal fancier and his family, who are commanded to build a boat in the middle of the desert.

The flood comes and goes. The entire population of the human and animal world are cooped up in a wooden box for just over a year, after which they understandably scarper. Then comes the long, complicated saga of God interfering with the progression of Man despite washing his hands of the lot of them in a confusing rainbow-laced pinky-swear. There are different languages everywhere, then there was only one, then there were none anywhere when God decided to destroy the Tower of Babel. Finally, a long bloody drama that would make Midsomer Murders look like Sesame Street. People are killed, lied to, defrauded, violated, damaged, mutilated, chucked in a hole and sold into slavery, deceived and otherwise behave abominably, because an invisible man in the sky told them to do it. Well, okay, perhaps back then he wasn't entirely invisible. Perhaps back then there was a hyper-advanced humanoid floating about, dictating life and death over the lesser humanoids he had created to relieve a fit of boredom. We weren't there, so I guess we'll never really know the truth of it all beyond the myriad interpretations of a 6,000-year-old game of Chinese Whispers. And that's pretty much it.

And now, let us continue our journey, starting with the ramblings of Exodus and progressing to whatever passage we reach where I lose interest and end the book. Take each passage as it comes, I say, so long as it makes for an invigorating, fun-filled read. Let us resume!

Exodus 1: Everybody hates Israelites

"To read the bible without horror, we must undo every thing that is tender, sympathizing and benevolent in the heart of man." -Thomas Paine, The Age of Reason

We resume our journey pretty much where we left off, with a quick recap of the descendants of Jacob/Israel/whatever (I knew there'd be at least one reference to that multi-named individual – let's just grit our teeth and move on with it) and numbers and lines, and so forth. We hear that Joseph and all of his generation have died, yet the Israelites have become exceedingly fruitful. Hardly a surprise there, considering Joseph was holding the meta-phorical reins of Egypt and had set up his rellies with the most fertile land in the country (Gen. 47:6, in case you were wondering). And all is well, until a new king came to power in Egypt – not a pharaoh, but a king this time, who didn't know Joseph from a bar of pro-verbial soap. So, this new king gathers his high-up homies and whines that the Israelites have *"become far too numerous for us"* (Ex. 1:9), fearing that they will become even more numerous, join with Egypt's enemies, fight against them and leave the country. Typical paranoid behaviour endemic of any ruling personage, really. His solution was to appoint slave-masters to oppress the Israelites with forced labour, creating the cities of Pithom and Rameses for the Pharaoh (back to Pharaoh now, not king – Ex.1:11). Regular readers will be very familiar with this interchanging of names and position titles, so if you are a new reader, do be aware that this is just a "thing" the bible does, and we just have to roll with it as and when it occurs.

Anyway, all this hard labour business doesn't seem to be affecting the Israelite population growth, so the king (back to king) tells the Hebrew midwives to kill the male offspring of any Hebrew women, but to let the female offspring live (Ex. 1:16). Needless to say, the midwives were having none of it, and allowed the males to live. Now, if this pharaoh/king had two brain cells to throw in with his paranoid genocidal mania, he would have ordered the females killed, the males castrated for slaves, and the Israelites would have been eradicated in one generation. Instead, he was thinking with his loins and the prospect of future sex-slaves, which may explain in part why Judaism is matrilineal in nature.

The king was pissed at being baulked by the midwives, but they explained that Hebrew women were "vigorous" and gave birth before they could arrive, sparing them from the executioner's block. His next brilliant idea is to tell the populace that all male Hebrew births were to be chucked in the river, while still sparing the females. Randy old king.

Exodus 2: The Birth of Moses

"There aren't just bad people that commit genocide; we are all capable of it. It's our evolutionary history." -James Lovelock

Now pay attention here, guys, because the people represented in this passage are largely represented by pronouns only; so, if you're not careful, you can end up spending several hours trying to figure out who is whom. Never fear, though, dearest readers, for I have already, graciously, wasted those hours for you. You're welcome..!

We begin in the usual manner, in that a Levite dude married a Levite chick, got jiggy with it and ended up with a son; and after determining that he *"was a fine child, she hid him for three months"* (Ex. 2:1). After this, it apparently became impossible to hide the child, so she made a basket of papyrus and coated it in tar and pitch, tossed the kid inside and stuffed the basket in among the reeds in the Nile (Ex. 2:3). Then we read, *"His sister stood at a distance to see what would happen to him"* (Ex. 2:4). There was no mention of a sister, or indeed of any births prior to the kid in the basket, so what's going on here?

Further digging about reveals that Basket Boy is actually the third-born child, with another boy,

Aaron, who is three years older; and a girl, Miriam, who is six years older. The three month hiding period we read about here stems from Exodus 1, where the Pharaoh/King/whatever put out the decree to kill all the male Hebrew babies. This was apparently effected by the royal troops knocking down the door of newly-wed couples nine months after they registered as married and searching for illicit progeny (as well as being guided by the screams of babies of course). So, if we go along those lines, either Basket-boy's mother only carried him for six months, or she was three months into her pregnancy when she married, the latter making more sense if she was expecting her door to be kicked down by the royal baby killers.

So. Three months old now, chucked inna basket and shoved into the reeds in the river and left there, but with a sister in the wings, watching. Now we hear that the Pharaoh's daughter came down with her attendant slave girls for a bath and discovered Basket Boy, getting one of her slaves to retrieve it. She (I presume Pharaoh's daughter) opened the basket and took pity on the kid, and identified him as a Hebrew child. Now, I'm no expert on these things, but I can guarantee without even being there that she wasn't making that conclusion based on the "blanket in the basket" as is suggested in the movies, but rather "the bob job on the nob," if you'll pardon the colourful parlance.

It was at this point that Blanket Boy's sister Miriam swooped down on the group and asked if she should run and grab a Hebrew woman to wet-nurse the kid (Ex. 2:7) which was agreed to, and so Miriam went and fetched Basket Boy's mother. She was then given the baby and told to, *"Take his baby and nurse it for me, and I will pay you"* (Ex. 2:9). This was done and then, when the kid grew older, he was taken to the Pharaoh's daughter for adoption (Ex. 2:10) and named Moses, saying "I drew him out of the water".

A pretty sweet swindle, don't you think? If we ignore for a moment the infanticide that created the situation in the first place, we have a kid (well three kids, really) born out of wedlock, hidden from sight and sound for three months, then thrown in the river; only to be found by the pharaoh's daughter no less, who falls for a cunning ruse formulated by a six-year-old child to keep the baby in the arms of its mother (and getting PAID for it, no less!), and finally to be adopted into the royal pharaoh family! To all those people who are cheating Centrelink to get more welfare payments, this should be a clear indication that you need to step up your game if you want to trump this kid's acumen.

And while we're on the subject of avoiding the pharaoh's baby killers, why (and how) is Aaron still alive? He would have been considered an infant almost up to Moses' birth, so how exactly did he dodge his post-natal swimming classes? "Naah, sorry guv, you can't take Aaron and chuck him in the river. He's got a cold, you see, the doctor says he's gotta stay out of the water or he'll catch his death..." Somehow, I don't think that argument would work; and there is a complete lack of explanation as to how Aaron can be running about all Male Hebrew and shit while his kid brother is being hunted down for termination.

So, who was this infanticidal pharaoh? While we are often told that it was Ramesses II who was on the throne at the time of the flight of the Hebrews into the desert, he was also step-brother to Moses, so we can only really assume that it was Ramesses II's father who was responsible for this, who was Seti I. However, aside from a passing reference to this in the 1998 animated film, "The Prince of Egypt," there is no mention in the historical archives to suggest he ordered the infanticide. I mean, sure, it's not something you want included in your resume if you can help it, but you would think that something as extreme as this would pop up somewhere other than in a book of fables and the associated study groups. There seems to be no independent evidence to verify these claims and so, as I am wont to do in situations like these, I did the Math.

Exodus would have us believe that Moses was step-brother to Ramesses II, and that when Ramesses II assumed the throne, Moses started his god-plague business to convince him to, "Let My People Go...!!!" or words to that effect. According to my esteemed colleagues Google and Wikipedia, Ramesses II was born in 1303BC and died 90 years later in 1213BC. Moses, however, is alleged to have been born in 1527BC and died 120 years later in 1407BC – which means that Moses died 104 years *before* Ramesses II was even born. Awkward....! Furthermore, if you put Moses' birthdate into the timeline of Egyptian pharaohs, it indicates that Ahmose I was sitting on the throne at the time and – surprise, surprise! – no mention of any infanticidal tendencies there, either. If the date is to be believed, then Moses saw the rise and fall of no less than seven pharaohs in his lifetime, dying during the reign of Amenhotep II.

Moses, however, has an alibi in a second set of life dates, those being 1391BC – 1271BC. If we run with those figures, we discover that it was either Thutmose IV or Amenhotep III on the throne depending on when succession occurred versus when Moses was born. In this second available range of dates, Ramesses II was alive at the time to have known about his step-brother, although there were still at least ten pharaohs in this range of dates (eleven if you count the change of reign at Moses' time of birth). Looking a little deeper, however, we can see that Moses was already 88 years old – and eight years into his 40-year desert trek - when Ramesses II was born. Ramesses assumed the throne in his 29th year (1274BC), and Moses died three years later in 1271BC. This means we are led to believe that as soon as Ramesses II sat down, Moses was in his face with all manner of plagues and such in an effort to free his people; and that finally after ten such plagues, Ramesses II relented and let Moses' people go.

Now here's the rub: Assuming that all of this plague nonsense occurred in the year of his coronation, it means that Moses freed the slaves in 1274BC at the very earliest, and then dies just three years later. But hang on a minute: he still has *forty years of wandering* to do yet! To say nothing of climbing up and down Mt. Sinai, lugging heavy stone tablets, talking to burning bushes, cursing his people for false idolatry, et cetera. No wonder there is so much truth to the axiom that, "those who believe in the bible have never actually read it."

Random Sidenote: Those of you who read my previous book on this subject will recall the bible's inability to accurately establish proper timelines for the events contained therein, and the efforts taken to reconcile them. So, for shits and giggles (and because I am such a complete shithead), I took Moses' remaining forty years and divided it up into thirteen lunar months, which gave me an answer of 3.07 solar years – the exact amount of time between Ramesses II assuming the throne and the death of Moses. Isn't maths fun, kids? But before the creationists among you get too excited by that example of serendipity, bear in mind that to make the math work you would need to put Moses' age into the same equation, which put his death at age nine – far too young to be organizing a Hebrew rebellion. Although, if anyone is going to curse you with plagues of gnats, boils and frogs, it would probably be a six-year-old child.

Moses Murders a Mofo

Okay, so I got a little carried away with doing the math again, so we'll shake our heads clear of that - for now – and resume our analysis. The second portion of this verse/chapter begins with, *"One day, after Moses had grown up, he went out to where his own people were and watched them at their hard labour"* (Ex. 2:11). Yeeah, sorry, I sense more Math approaching. *"After Moses had grown up,"* we are told. How old, exactly, would that be? Let us read on: *"He saw an Egyptian beating a Hebrew, one of his own people. Looking this way and that and seeing no one, he killed the Egyptian and hid him in the sand"* (Ex. 2:11-2:12). Sooo, if he's old enough to beat an Egyptian guard to death, it's safe to assume he's in his early twenties and not, say, three. Okay, that's out of my system, moving on. The next day he sees a couple of his Hebe homies fighting each other, and exhorts them to stop, asking one, *"Why are you hitting your fellow Hebrew?"* He replied, *"Who made you ruler and judge over us? Are you thinking of killing me as you killed the Egyptian?"* (Ex. 2:13 – 2:14). At this point, Moses shits himself thinking that he was seen offing the guard, and he was right: when the Pharaoh got wind of it, he ordered Moses to be killed, but Moses managed to high-tail it out of the country and ended up by a well in some place called Midian. While he was there, he rescued a group of women who were trying to water their flocks from a bunch of arsehole shepherds who were trying to drive them off. After which, he watered the flocks for them and eventually got invited back to meet their father, and then got hitched to one of the daughters, Zipporah. In time, she popped out a son they called Gershom, meaning something stupid like, *"I have become a foreigner in a foreign land"* (Ex. 2:22). Anyway, all this happened during which the pharaoh died – exactly which one is up for debate – and the Israelites cried out in their misery and suffering and shit, so loudly that God heard it. Now, *"God heard their groaning and remembered his covenant with Abraham, with Isaac and with Jacob. So God looked*

upon the Israelites and was concerned about them"
(Ex. 2:24 – 2:25).

I call bullshit. If God was so concerned about the plight of his people, surely it would have been within his omnipotent ability to simply smite the pharaoh and his family before giving Egypt to the Israelites. Why was it even remotely necessary for God to let his "chosen people" suffer at the hands of the Egyptians? A quick point of his finger, zap!, the pharaoh is now a few scattered molecules, the witnesses go, "oohh!" and everything is sorted. No mysterious signs, no broken promises, just do what I command and I won't fry your arses. This time. Perhaps. I only promised it wouldn't be water again. Worship me!!!!

Exodus 3: Moses Beats Around the Bush

"Every few thousand years some shepherd inhales smoke from a burning bush and has a vision or eats moldy rye bread in a cave and sees God." -Kerry Thornley.

As you may have guessed from the witty play on words above, in this chapter Moses comes across a bush near Horeb, colloquially called the Mountain of God (is Onanism still a Thing? If it is, let's hope he said sorry afterward). He said to himself, *"I will go over and see this strange sight – why the bush does not burn up"* (Ex. 3:3). As it turns out, God was sneaky-watching him going toward this bush, and called out from within the flames, *"Moses! Moses!"* (Ex. 3:4).

Immediately, I'm going to ask why God hasn't told him his name isn't now Jeff or Glenn or Grrglflurg or some other weird made-up name as was his penchant in Genesis (Side note: Seriously, ladies: who in their right mind carries a baby in their womb for nine months, gives painful birth to it and then after all that effort, calls it Glenn..?!) The second question I have is why God has decided to use this method of arboreal communication instead of just walking up to him or using his holographic array (see my first book if you haven't already for my explanation of holograms). Legend suggests to us that the everburning bush was a species of acacia, many of which are known to contain psychoactive alkaloids which are released in the smoke when burned. It is entirely probable that Moses was stoned off his tits from the smoke and was talking to the voices inside his own head; but that would make for a very short book, and to be honest it's quite fun to insert some modern-day explanations into these things. Anyway, God conjures this weird burning bush method of communication from which he can project his voice to Moses, if only to make himself seem more enigmatic. Not that it matters, really. But just for giggles, a quick search for Mt. Sinai on Google maps led me to a mountain range in Saudi Arabia with the unlikely name of Jabal Mousa (natives to the language could probably tell you what that means, although the general theme here is, "Mountain of God") for its blackened peak and a rock Moses supposedly split to let the water out and so on. I also found an interesting entry for Mt. Horeb on a site called Atlas Obscura, which told me that the entire mountain is surrounded by barbed wire and patrolled by armed Saudi guards, so *"getting too close is out of the question,"* quote-unquote. Pardon me for being so openly querulous here, but why would an omnipotent, omnipresent God need his hill wrapped in barbed wire and guarded by armed security? If God didn't want us on his hill, then surely he could deal with the errant trespasser himself with a minimum of fuss? Ex. 19:12 puts it down plainly enough: *"Put limits for people around the mountain and tell them, 'Be careful that you do not approach the mountain or touch the foot of it. Whoever touches the mountain is to be put to death."* Well sure, but I still feel God should be dealing with trespassers himself; it kinda lends some credibility to the whole omnipotent thing.

Anyway, carrying on. G-man and Moses are up in the mountain rapping with each other, and after making Moses take off his sandals, God starts bullshitting about how concerned he is for his Chosen People's suffering. He says that he has come down to rescue them from the hands of the Egyptians and bring them out into the Land of Milk and Honey – currently home to the Canaanites, Hittites, Amorites, Hivites, Jebusites and a couple more tribes. Setting up more dodgy Air-BnB deals to slot his Chosen Peeps into homes to which they have no claim, again! He states all that, and then God says, *"So now, go. I am sending you to Pharaoh to bring my people the Israelites out of Egypt"* (Ex. 3:10). Moses is all like, "Who am I that I should do it?" and rightly so, considering he was on the run from the previous pharaoh and it's highly likely that this death warrant hasn't been rescinded with the coronation of the new one, who should now be Ramesses II if we set any store in the bible's dodgy timeline. He killed an Egyptian, and that is unlikely to be forgiven in a hurry.

God then tells Moses, *"I will be with you. And this will be the sign to you that it is I who have sent you: When you have brought the people out of Egypt, you will worship God on this mountain"* (Ex. 3:12). So.... Moses' sign from God that he is the one to do this Thing, is that he will do this Thing, then worship God on his mountain? A pretty cyclic argument, if you ask me, and both a self-fulfilling and self-defeating argument at that. You brought the peeps out of Egypt? Woah, that's your sign, totally called it, dude! What, you didn't do the Thing? Aaah, see, you didn't believe / you missed the sign / God was just screwing with you (circle most applicable). God can claim Moses was either bestowed with divine Destiny, or dismiss the whole thing by saying Moses wasn't pious enough or doubted too much and lost his divine blessing, ensuring a win no matter the outcome. Dodgy thinking if I've ever seen it.

Moses drifts by that though, and asks, *"Well, suppose I do this Thing and tell them 'the God of your fathers has sent me to you,' and they ask me, 'What is his name?'"* (Ex. 3:13); and by way of an answer, God replied, *"God said to Moses, 'I AM WHO I AM. This is what you are to say to the Israelites: "I AM has sent me to you"* (Ex. 3:14).

I am who I am..?! "I am" has sent me? Really?! Moses wasn't asking for your wifi password or your fucking PIN, dude, he just needs a name!

To help put just a modicum of credibility into an outrageous story! I really couldn't help myself here, so I had a look for some Hebrew writing or, more accurately, an alphabetized form of it, so that I could make some sense of this frankly batshit-mental reply from God. What I found was both interesting and amusing in equal measure.

It wasn't long before I found a ready-reckoner chart that compared letters based on their Latin, Hebrew, Aramaic and Greek roots respectively; however, I was only interested in the Hebrew (because, after all, we're referring to the God of Hebrews here, so it makes sense that any orders would be written down in that language). My attention was immediately drawn to two letters in particular:

- "M" – imagine a small letter w with a large comma attached to the right hand side;

- "N" – imagine a small letter v with the same comma attached to the right hand side.

If we take this information into consideration, and we allow for the possibility that the bible is open to interpretation (Ha..!), then what if,

"I AM WHO I AM. This is what you are to say to the Israelites: I AM has sent me to you."

is actually,

"IAN WHO I AM. This is what you are to say to the Israelites. IAN has sent me to you."

Or possibly, *"I AM WHO? IAN."* It depends on the inflections you use. The point I am making here is that some dude called Ian has been screwing with mankind for his own twisted amusement; and as a bonus prize we've been able to positively determine God's gender, because who calls their girl Ian? Anyway, God (Ian) spouts some more rubbish about yea verily, you'll lead them out of Egypt and more Land of Milk and Honey claims and so on and so forth. Another bit about Moses being told that he and the Israelite elders will go to the king of Egypt and propose, *"a three-day journey into the wilderness to offer sacrifices to the LORD our God"* (Ex. 3:18). Well, okay, I don't think that'll happen, because God's already said that the pharaoh is a tough cookie; he's not about to just get up and walk off into the desert on his slaves' behest. Then God tells Moses that he'll make all the Egyptians "favourably disposed" to them, and tells Moses to make every woman ask their neighbours for items of silver and gold and clothing, to put it all on their sons and daughters, and thus plunder the Egyptians. (Ex. 3:21 – 3:22). Yeah, sure, that'll work ... not! One of the things about items made out of silver and gold is that, by and large, people make great efforts not to part with them. Additionally, it is at odds with Jacob's demand that his followers take off all their gold and baubles and give them to him to bury under an oak tree in Shechem back in Gen. 35. I mean, really: first God wants his peeps to be "purified" of all these material trappings, and now he wants them to out-bling Mr. T. - you can't have it both ways, Ian, so pick a struggle, already...!

THE BIBLE - ALPHABETS							
	Hebrew						Syr
OV		ARL	TNR	NV	P	Name	
13	מ	ם מ	ם מ	40	M	Mem	ܩ
14	ﬥ	ן נ	ן נ	50	N	Nun	ܢ
15	‡	ס	ס	60	S	Samekh	ܣ
16	O	ע	ע	70	(o)	Ayin	ܥ
17	ﬤ	ף פ	ף פ	80	P, F	Pe	ܦ

Hebrew characters for, "M" and "N" respectively, showing how a person with an excitable imagination (and/or a chisel) could quite easily misinterpret (or screw about with) ancient texts. Isn't that right, "I AM" ... or should I say, "Ian?"

Exodus 4: Moses practices his magic tricks, returns to Egypt

"The genre of Fantasy is about magic and occult characters." –Shawn Ashmore

This passage finds Moses still having difficulty with the assignment God (Ian) has tasked to him, and like Crazy Ol' Abe before him, presses the G-man for more details and assurances. I can't say I blame him, owing to his unresolved fugitive status back in Egypt and a lack of solid evidence that he is who he claims to be beyond, "because God said I was." Which, to be honest, carried as much weight back then as it would today, i.e. absolutely none.

He begins the passage by asking, *"What if they don't believe me or listen to me and say, 'The LORD did not appear to you'?"* (Ex. 4:1). Predictably, God replies, *"What is that in your hand?"* (Ex. 4:2). Okay, firstly, that sounded like a cheesy attention-deflecting statement you might hear from a bad stage magician or an orange president; ooh, what's that behind your ear, do you always keep shekels back there, you must be worth a fortune! Secondly, God is supposed to be omniscient, so how could he *not* know what Moses had in his hand? Not doing very well in the all-seeing, all-knowing department are we, Ian? If you can't even see what's right in front of your glowy face, then good luck seeing what's in my mind and heart, is all I can say.

So anyway, it was a staff. Moses predictably replies, "A staff." So, God tells him to throw it on the ground (which he does) and it turns into a snake, making Moses shit his 'ezor and run away screaming. After a hearty laugh (and who wouldn't?) God tells Moses to grab the tail of the snake, and when he eventually does it turns back into a staff. God is all like, "That'll prove you've been talking to me," and then he tells Moses to put his hand inside his cloak (Ex. 4:6). He does so, and when he takes it out again it had become leperous, and *"as white as snow."* Kinda hard to run from that trick, I'll grant you. God tells Moses to put his hand in his cloak again and he finds his hand restored to normal. And God's all like, *"If they do not believe you or pay attention to the first sign, they will believe the second"* (Ex. 4:8). God then provides a fallback miracle for him and tells Moses to take some water from the Nile and, *"pour it on the dry ground. The water you take from the river will become blood on the ground"* (Ex. 4:9).

Ah yes, the water into blood thing. Quite a fun thing if you know the trick of it, and it *is* a trick, relying on a knowledge of the Nile and its cycle of ebbs and flows, and what is happening with your environment. Put simply, you're looking at an algal bloom, but not just any old garden-variety algae. In particular, planktothrix rubescens, which thrives when the Nile is slow-moving and muddy and combined with rising ambient temperatures. It's not much of a stretch to presume that, while the waters of the Nile could still be normal in colour, grabbing a gourdful and pouring it on dry sand would effectively filter out the water as it soaks in and concentrate the algae, to the effect that you would end up with a gooey red mess on the ground strongly resembling blood. But if that theory doesn't float your boat, there is another natural cause for this with the Chromatiaceae bacteria, which is the main family of purple sulphur bacteria, and can bloom during times of environmental change such as a drought (and we already know there was such an event, back when Joseph made like a squirrel after God warned him of a severe drought and famine). In short, when the water became stagnant and deoxygenated, the bacteria would thrive on the dying fish and produce a stink not unlike that reported in the scriptures. In fact, do yourselves a favour and put "Plagues of Egypt" into your Wikipedia search, and see for yourself how the plagues (and in particular, the order of them) can be explained in a completely rational and logical manner. It really is worth a read, so I'll just wait here until you get back. Dum-de-dummm… *whistles tunelessly*….

You're back? Coolio! Let's crack on, shall we? So now we have Moses arguing his lack of eloquence, and that he is *"slow of speech and tongue"* (Ex. 4:10). And God is all like, who do

33

you think gave humans their mouths, and tells Moses that he will coach him and teach him the things to say and how to say it. Mind you, he also claimed to have given humans hearing and sight and other cool things that are generally credited to Evolution. But then, if the concept of a Space-faring species kickstarting our own has any merit, it *could* be argued that God gave us the power of speech and higher intelligence. Moses, however, is still crying off from his holy quest, and requests God to, *"please send someone else"* (Ex. 4:13). God finally loses his shit with Moses and says, *"What about your brother, Aaron the Levite? I know he can speak well; you will put words in his mouth … and I will teach you both what to say and do. He will speak for you … as if you were God to him"* (Ex. 4:14 – 4:16), but to be sure they took the staff with them so they could perform their magic tricks.

Moses returns to Egypt

Running back to his father-in-law, Moses asks him if he can sod off back to Egypt to see if any of his peeps are still alive. Perhaps thinking he was referring to his brothers, parents, whatever, he let Moses go with his blessing. So, with God stepping in briefly to tell him that everyone who wanted to kill him in Egypt was dead, he packed up his wife and kids onto a donkey and hoofed it back to Egypt, remembering to also take the Staff of God™ with him. All good so far.

Now we read something that would make any self-respecting human stop dead in their donkey tracks and abandon the quest then and there. To wit: *"The LORD said to Moses, 'When you return to Egypt, see that you perform before Pharaoh all the wonders I have given you the power to do. **But I will harden his heart so that he will not let the people go'.**"* (Ex. 4:21).

What.... THE-fuck?! You have to be burdened with a major mental malfunction to think this is a rational course of action! Why would God even bother to help his Chosen People if he was going to white-ant the efforts of the person he chose to set them free? "Okay, yeah, Moses, you go and show pharaoh your awesome magic powers I've given you so that my people can go free ... but just to make it interesting, I'm going to turn the pharaoh into an obstinate arsehat so he won't let those people go." Sounds legit.

And moreover, make it interesting for whom? Certainly not any of the players on the mortal plane, that's for sure. Sounds to me like God is back to his old tricks, making humanity jump through his hoops for his own sick and twisted amusement. There's simply no other way to interpret this self-defeating course of action. And you know, if the pharaoh was the source of angst with God's Chosen Peeps, it would probably have been much simpler to oooh, I dunno, zap him into ash with his smitey-finger of doom, perhaps? It's so much more effective than giving a magic walking stick to a renegade Hebrew, it proves your existence and it sends a clear message not to mess with his fave peeps. But no, let's do it the long winded, far more complicated way because God has an eternity to kill and it'll keep him amused for a short while.

Now readers, if you think what you just read is strange, well ho ho! Just you wait for this bit! It makes a psychopath's behaviours look normal by comparison; but as always, I shall relay the facts and mark the passages, and you can make up your own minds on this. God tells Moses to go to the pharaoh and say, *"'This is what the LORD says: Israel is my firstborn son, and I told you, "Let my son go, so he may worship me." But you refused to let him go, so I will kill your firstborn son.'"* (Ex.4:22). Followed by, *"At a lodging place, the LORD met Moses and was about to kill him. But Zipporah took a flint knife, cut off her son's foreskin and touched Moses' feet with it"* and God left him alone (Ex. 4:24 – 4:26).

Yep..! That's what it says, alright.

First of all, why the hell would you try and kill the person you've selected to champion your quest to rescue your chosen people?! How completely out-to-lunch to you have to be to consider that a rational thing to do? Let's just pause for the sake of clarity and review these events slowly, shall we?

- God's peeps are being oppressed by the pharaoh;
- God recruits Moses as his champion to rescue the peeps from the pharaoh;
- God then turns pharaoh into a prick to make Moses' mission harder;
- God tries to kill Moses enroute for no apparent reason;
- Moses' wife carves up his son's junk and wipes it on Moses' feet;
- God goes, 'Eeeeewww!' and runs away.

It's disturbing behaviour to say the least from a supposedly "all wise" god. On the positive side though, we have discovered God's kryptonite; if you think you're about to be killed by a mad Hebrew God, just hack of your kid's foreskin and rub it all over you. He'll be doing the Red Sea Skedaddle back to heaven before you can say Chutzpah. You'd have to find a way to live with what you've done to yourself and to your kid, of course, and you'd have a much smaller circle of friends, but at least you'd live.

Then there's the issue of the savaged sausage to account for. Considering that the Circumcision covenant is supposed to be performed on the

8th day (or thereabouts), it begs the question of why the kid had not, in fact, been circumcised prior to this event. An exhaustive search for names and dates proved unfruitful except for a rough timeline in Acts 7, basically saying Moses killed the Egyptian and fled when he was 40, married Zipporah and had two sons, lived in Midian for 40 years, and hopped it back to Egypt when he was 80 years old. Moses would not have waited forty years before doing the deed with Zipporah, so Gershom would have to have been in his thirties, at least. So we have to presume the second child was the one being referred to in this passage, and whom for some reason wasn't circumcised by then.

Finally, you have to wonder about the mental math of Zipporah. I really want to know what her process was, to be able to go from, "God is killing my husband," to, "My husband's son isn't circumcised," to, "God hates foreskins," which culminated in her whipping out her son's wang for a flint flensing. To put all those things together in her head, in the limited time she had available to her, is nothing short of psychotic. And why a flint knife? Even as far back as 3000BCE, the Egyptians were expertly making weapons from bronze alloys, so there is no reason at all, over 1,500 years later, to be faffing about with a primitive flint knife! Perhaps it was an extra penance that fell upon the hapless second child for not getting his dong docked earlier: "Sorry son, God is royally pissed at your dad; so we're dispensing with the razor-sharp bronze knife in favour of the crappy flint one, and hopefully he'll overlook our lapse." Le Ouch.

Anyway, back to the narrative. God apparently appears before Aaron (Moses' brother) and tells him to meet Moses in the wilderness; he ends up meeting him at the foot of the Mountain of God (Sinai or Horeb as the case may be – I haven't been able to definitively establish which one it was at this time) and he kissed him. I don't know why it was necessary to include that detail, but whatever. Moses then laid down everything that had happened and all the signs they're supposed to perform, and after they gathered all the elders to them, Aaron relayed all the messages and they performed all the nice magic tricks, and the elders fell for it and believed God was actually concerned about their people and bowed down and worshipped (Ex. 4:27 – 4:31).

My first thought here is that, being elders, they would be wise. Isn't that the primary function of elders, to listen to troubles and impart their wisdom as required? Perhaps Moses and Aaron embellished the facts just a tiny bit, leaving out the bits that pointed to the fact that God was a complete fruitcake. We weren't there, so we are unable to verify this with any accuracy; but if I was an elder, and told of these antics, I think I would be a little more skeptical, and a little bit worried that we had a mentally unstable being of advanced power running about meddling in the affairs of Men. It's not the kind of thing that instills confidence in your continuing existence, that's for sure. A moot point, though, because Aaron and Moses managed to convince them that God was on their side, and that's where we leave this particular chapter.

Exodus 5: Moses Ain't Winning Friends

"The most potent weapon of the oppressor is the mind of the oppressed." -Steven Biko

In what promises to be another confusing verse, Moses approaches the pharaoh with his – well, God's – demands to let the Israelites go, so that they can hold a festival in the wilderness (Ex. 5:1). Pharaoh apparently replied, *"Who is the LORD, that I shall obey him and let Israel go? I do not know the LORD and I will not let Israel go"* (Ex. 5:2). So, who (or what) is Israel? It surely can't mean Moses' son, who is supposed to be travelling with his old man, despite there being slightly less of him now than when they departed for Egypt. I don't think it means Israel the country, because how can you let a tract of land go to a festival in the wilderness? The best fit here would be "Israel" as representing the combined peoples of Israel, in particular the Hebrews. It's a pedantic thing I know, but why they can't use plain language is beyond me.

They then tell the pharaoh that they have met with "the God of the Hebrews", and invite him to come on a three-day journey into the wilderness to offer sacrifices, or, *"he may strike us with plagues or the sword"* (Ex. 5:3). So, what's the deal here? Is God once again corporeal in nature, or are we talking about a burning bush waving a scimitar about with deadly intent? Instead, the king (pharaoh) asks the pair why they are intent on taking the people away from their labour, tells them to get back to work, and tells the overseers to stop supplying straw for the bricks. Furthermore, the quota of bricks is not to be reduced, thinking that working them harder will prevent them from *"being lazy"* and then they will *"pay no attention to lies"* (Ex. 5:4 – 5:9).

The orders filter down to the line to the slaves, who now have to run around the countryside gathering their own straw for these bricks. The slave drivers then beat the Israelite overseers when they don't meet the quotas, and everyone is understandably pissed. Of course, the beaten overseers appeal to the Pharaoh, asking him a heartfelt, "WTF?" only to be told they were lazy and to get back to work and stop their god nonsense. The overseers go back (probably after another beating), track down Moses and his git brother and berate the pair for worsening the Hebrew suffering: *"May the LORD look on you and judge you! You have made us obnoxious to Pharaoh and have put a sword in their hand to kill us"* (Ex. 5:21). Well, you can't really blame them, can you: it's no different to today's work force, when you get that one idiot who says or does something stupid, and then everyone else suffers as a result, because the company has to cater for the Lowest Common Denominator. Instead of dealing with Moses and his brother directly, the Pharaoh makes broad sweeping policy designed to let Moses' own people do his dirty work for him, i.e. beat the bugger to death and get on with their indentured servitude.

Moses for his part *"returned to the LORD"* (what, all the way back to the burning bush..?) and asked why he's brought trouble upon his peeps: *"Ever since I went to Pharaoh to speak in your name, he has brought trouble on his people, and you have not rescued your people at all"* (Ex. 5:23). Well, this was not entirely unexpected, was it? God had already told Moses that he would harden the Pharaoh and turn him into a recalcitrant prick, so complaining about it isn't going to solve the problem. Just as he did with the Tower of Babel, God could have just come down and lifted his peeps out of their slavery and plopped them down anywhere he desired, but instead chose to screw with his chosen ones and make them jump through some hoops for his amusement. For an all-mighty and powerful god, he's not doing a hell of a lot to endear himself to his peeps. It's supposed to be one of the benefits of having a deity on your side: to care for your plight, to lift you out of adversity, to smite your foes, etc. But observing this god's behaviour, it's no wonder people started to find other things to worship and making up new gods to pray at. Given that there are over four thousand religions in practice today, there was obviously a lot of trial and error involved.

Exodus 6: God Deflects the Question

"We do not have to be mental health professionals to identify the traits of the possible sociopaths among us." -P.A. Speers

So we left Moses at God's bushstep, asking him why he was being such a prick to the people he is supposed to be rescuing from the Egyptians. God has obviously been watching Parliament Question Time in Moses' absence, because he starts off with, *"Now you'll see what I will do to Pharaoh: Because of my mighty hand he will let them go; because of my mighty hand he will drive them out of his country"* (Ex. 6:1). Yeah, believe it when I see it, buddy. God then goes on to brag that he, *"appeared to Abraham and Isaac and Jacob as God Almighty, but by my name the LORD I did not make myself fully known to them"* (Ex. 6:3). What the hell does that mean? You were either there or you weren't, dude. Genesis, if it is to be believed, clearly has you physically meddling in the affairs of men; breaking bread with Abe on the outskirts of Soddom; having moonlight-wrestling matches with Jacob/Israel/Whatever on the banks of some river before touching him inappropriately on the hip tendon; and even before that, walking with Noah and devising plans to drown the earth's population. That's as "fully known" as most people would ever want to be with a demonstrably psychopathic god, I reckon, but whatever.

God then rambles on about his famous Canaan Covenant which still hasn't been fulfilled at this stage of the game (Side Note: did that covenant EVER get fulfilled? I'm not entirely up to speed with middle-eastern politics, but I'm fairly sure people are still fighting over that particular stretch of land), that he's heard the "groaning" of the Israelites, that he has remembered this covenant, and then oddly states, *"I will take you as my own people, and I will be your God. Then you will know that I am the LORD your God, who brought you out from under the yoke of the Egyptians"* (Ex. 6:7). I mean, it's already been stated that the Israelites are God's Chosen Ones so I don't understand why he needs to reclaim ownership of them. It's like owning your car for twenty years, and then claiming that you WILL take the car as your own, and that you will be its driver; it's complete and utter nonsense!

God goes on and claims (re-claims) transference of Canaan that, *"I swore with uplifted hand to give to Abraham, to Isaac and to Jacob"* (Ex. 6:8). Okay so he's forgotten – *again* – that he had renamed Jacob to Israel after his nocturnal tumble by the river, but that's beside the point: the "uplifted hand" indicates that "God" at some stage of the game was perceived as a corporeal being, and not some burning bush or brain hemorrhage in the perceiver. A being of superior abilities and technologies but also burdened with some serious mental and ethical deficiencies if the biblical account so far is any indication.

So, Moses heads back to Egypt and relays all these ramblings to the Israelites, who quite understandably refuse to listen because the last time they did, it got them harder labour and more whippings from the slave masters. Then, *"the LORD said to Moses, 'Go, tell the Pharaoh to let the Israelites go out of this country'"* (Ex. 6:10 – 6:11). Soooo, God was in Egypt now? Or did Moses hightail it back to the mountain bush for more guidance? Moses for his part asked that, if the Israelites won't listen to him, what made God believe the Pharaoh would listen, as he *"spoke with faltering lips"* (Ex. 6:12).

A good question, that. It's pretty hard to be a figurehead for your people if your own people think you're a prat. And God does answer, sort of, but first we're treated to a passage outlining the genealogy of the Moses line. Quite why it was necessary to put it in the middle of the narrative like that, I have no idea. Perhaps as a distraction technique to break the reader's concentration on the "facts" at hand, to better hide the obvious flaws in the script? It doesn't really matter; it's mainly boring stuff that you can look at in your own time; the only bit that is interesting is that of Amram, who in true Abrahamic family tradition married his father's sister Jochebed, who then bore him Moses and

Aaron (Ex. 6:20). It kinda tells you all you need to know about those two, doesn't it? Oh, and Aaron ended up having four kids to some chick called Elisheba, the older two being Nahab and Abihu (Abby who..?). More like, "whoopie-do." Anyway, we pick up the narrative a little further down where it reiterates the previous question with, *"Now when the LORD spoke to Moses in Egypt, he said to him, 'I am the LORD, tell Pharaoh king of Egypt everything I tell you'"* (Ex. 6:28 – 6:29), and another "faltering-lips" reply from Moses. So, God *was* in Egypt pissing in Moses' ear, and not ensconced in a fiery bush on some mountain-side as hitherto claimed. Good to know he's up and running about the place, "finding his thirty" so to speak. I can tell you're waiting with baited breath to find out what happens next; and for that, we'll have to start the next chapter. Onward and upward, as they say!

Exodus 7: Of Bitey Sticks and Bloody Plagues

"We are a plague on the Earth." -Sir David Attenborough

God kicks off this paragraph (and our long-awaited answer) by telling Moses, *"See, I have made you like God to Pharaoh, and your brother Aaron will be your prophet"* (Ex. 7:1). Actually, G-man, no we *don't* see. All we have seen so far is you cherry-picking some poor nervous sap of dubious genealogy and made him hop through some very unfair hoops for your amusement. But okay, let's give him the benefit of the doubt and see where he's going with this. God then tells the pair to tell the Pharaoh everything he commands them to, but will again harden the Pharaoh's heart despite multiplying "signs and wonders" in Egypt, so that he will not listen to them. Then God will strike Egypt with *"mighty acts of judgment"* and the people will be free and so on and so forth and yadda yadda yadda (7:2 – 7:5). At this stage, we are told that Moses was eighty years old, and Aaron eighty-three, when they spoke to the Pharaoh, commonly accepted to have been Ramesses II and earlier recognized to have ascended to Egypt's throne in 1474BCE, a mere three years before the alleged death of Moses in 1471BCE, who still had to free the Israelites *and* do forty years of wandering the desert. Go figure.

Anyhoo, God commands the pair to head off to the Pharaoh and tell him to let his people go, and the God-hardened Pharaoh refuses to listen to them. When they were asked by the Pharaoh to, "perform a miracle," they threw Moses' staff on the ground and it became a snake (Ex. 7:10). The Pharaoh responded with his own staff of wise men and sorcerers and replicated the act with their own staves; however we are led to believe that Moses' staff summarily consumed the staff-snakes of those notables. And so, the Pharaoh's heart became hard – hard*er* – and he would not let the people go.

So, we come now to the Plague of Blood. God gets into Moses' head again and tells him to go and confront the Pharaoh when he heads down to the Nile to do his morning ablutions or swim or whatever it was kings of Egypt were wont to do in those times. Whatever. He tells Moses to confront him and tell him that, *"the Lord has sent me to say to you: Let my people go, so that they may worship me in the wilderness. But until now you have not listened"* (Ex. 7:16). Well, considering God himself is making the guy deaf to Moses' demands, it's amusing to say the least. Further: *"With the staff that is in my hand I will strike the water of the Nile, and it will be changed into blood. The fish will die, and the river will stink; the Egyptians will not be able to drink its water"* (Ex. 7:17 – 7:18). Okay, so Moses is threatening to personally poison the water supply, got it. Then the very next verse: *"The LORD said to Moses, 'Tell Aaron: take your staff and stretch out your hand over the waters of Egypt … and they will turn to blood. Blood will be everywhere in Egypt, even in vessels of wood and stone'"* (Ex. 7:19). So it was Aaron, not Moses, who did this little deed. Exactly why Moses couldn't just dip the stick in the water himself is intriguing as it requires no language skills to achieve; and a "feeble tongue and mind" will not lessen the efficacy of the act, in spite of Moses getting all up in Pharaoh's face himself and reading the riot act to him without so much as a stammer. Are we to take from this that Moses was "cured" of his feeble mind and tongue for the duration of these acts, or was he just saying that to get out of doing it? It's difficult to tell without actually being there, so we'll tuck that little inconsistency away for later reference and move on with the narrative.

So they (well, Aaron) did the magic stick trick with the Nile, all the water turned into blood and the Egyptians were without water. And because we've already covered it, we know that it was most likely a period of drought and slow, stagnant water that increased the amount of the planktothrix rubescens bacteria to saturation point, leaching the oxygen out of the river water and making the fish die, improving the smell not one bit.

"Ahh, but what about the pots and vessels?!" I hear you scream. Easy enough: those pots and vessels were undoubtedly used, and regularly, to retrieve water from the river, in which case they would also be contaminated with the river bacteria. And as pots and vessels are smaller in volume than a river, it doesn't take long for the contents of that vessel to heat up the water such that the bacteria can flourish, especially in a hot climate like Egypt. So there's no great mystery how the pots and vessels were also affected.

This part, however, *is* interesting: *"But the Egyptian magicians did the same thing by their secret arts, and Pharaoh's heart became hard; he would not listen to Moses and Aaron, just as the LORD had said"* (Ex. 7:22). How, exactly, did the Egyptian magicians perform the same trick when *all the water had already been turned into blood?* Did they turn it back into water, and return it again to its bloody state? And if they were able to achieve that, why didn't they just *leave it as water*, nullifying the curse of this upstart Hebrew God before it could affect the people, gaining their admiration and securing the pharaoh in his position as supreme ruler, touched by obviously more powerful Egyptian gods? Instead, we are supposed to believe that the magicians performed the same acts, and just left it as blood for a week; it doesn't make any sense whatsoever! These magicians were in the Pharaoh's employment to counter any mystical attacks that may have been encountered; and if I'm not mistaken, having your drinking water turned into blood by a mad Hebrew god would qualify as a crisis to be nullified, not merely mirrored and ignored. Madness!

A little further on, another clue to our bloody dilemma: *"And all the Egyptians dug along the Nile to get drinking water, because they could not drink the water of the river"* (Ex. 7:24). If we cast our minds back to Ex. 4:9, Moses was originally told to take some water from the river and pour it on the sand, turning it into blood. Because, of course, the liquid part of the water would seep into the desert sands leaving the gooey red bacterial badness behind. The very fact that the Egyptian people dug along the river's banks to get fresh water puts paid to this theory, as the water table near the Nile would be sufficiently close to the surface to reach with minimal effort, and the straining effect of the sand on the Nile waters, particularly that below the surface which was choked with red algal bloom, means that the water would have been sufficiently treated to be able to drink safely. Which, of course, makes a liar out of the original Ex. 7:19 in that *all* of the water in Egypt had turned into blood. Well actually, no, obviously not. Sorry..!

Oh, and then seven days passed (Ex. 7:25).

Exodus 8: Heere, Froggy-Froggy-Froggy!!

"Theories pass. The frog remains." -Jean Rostand

Moses and his bro rock up to the Pharaoh again and again implore him to *"Let my people go,"* and that if he doesn't, *"I will send a plague of frogs on your whole country"* (Ex. 8:2). Basically threatening frogs everywhere from bedpots to breadpans, and a few places besides. Pharaoh ain't buyin' it, as they say; and so, *"The LORD said to Moses, 'Tell Aaron: stretch your staff over the streams and canals and ponds, and make the frogs come up on the land of Egypt"* (Ex. 8:4). Once again, getting Aaron to wave the stick because he is "feeble of tongue." Ugh. Aaron performs the act, and there are frogs everywhere. Great.

And once again, the Pharaoh's magicians come out and replicate the frog trick. And once again, did they send the frogs back and make them reemerge from the water? And if they did, why didn't they just keep them there? I'm beginning to think the Pharaoh needs new magicians that can neutralize these plagues instead of merely copying them, but who am I to judge? This time, the Pharaoh summons the brothers and tells them to *"pray to the LORD to take the frogs away from me and my people, and I will let your people go to offer sacrifices to the LORD"* (Ex. 8:8). No hardening of the heart this time, at least not yet. Moses, feeble tongue and all, ripostes with, *"I leave to you the honour of setting the time for me to pray for you and your officials and your people that you and your houses may be rid of the frogs, except for those that remain in the Nile"* (Ex. 8:9).

Feeble tongue indeed, pff..! Anyway, Pharaoh is all like, "Tomorrow, dude," and Moses is all like, "Okay, no problemo." More accurately, *"The frogs will leave you and your houses, your officials and your people; they will remain only in the Nile"* (Ex. 8:11). Okay, important bit, that; the frogs will leave the houses of their own will. Okay? Good. Next contradiction coming right up. Moses prayed and cried out about all the bloody frogs everywhere, to the following effect: *"And the LORD did what Moses asked. The frogs died in the houses, in the courtyards and in the fields. They were piled into heaps, and the land reeked of them"* (Ex. 8:13 – 8:14). So, in actual fact the frogs did NOT leave the houses, at least not corporeally; if they did leave, it was only in a metaphysical sense which in no way solves the problem. The frogs were then piled up – by that quickest expedient called "housekeeping" – and were left to decompose in the hot sun, the smell second only to Noah's ark on the 29th day afloat.

So why did the frogs invade the land? Well, frogs are amphibious, of course, able to breathe both air and water; and when the Nile became stagnant and algae-choked, they scarpered away from the smell and the airless water to find new places to swim and frolic, to the grief of those living near the river. Frogs, however, also need to keep their skin moist; and without being able to find fresh water for their bodily needs, they began to dehydrate and die off in short order. Again, no real mystery here when you explore the logical causes of events such as this. Even such oddities over the years, like fish and frogs falling from the sky like rain, can easily be attributed to natural causes such as hurricanes and the like, sucking up fish from the ocean and hoisting them overland to eventually fall when the twisters lose their impetus and dissipate. It's just a matter of applying logic.

Where were we? Ah yes, dead frogs literally everywhere. So, the Pharaoh observed that the froggy plague was dying out and that things were improving, if not the smell; and he hardened his heart (again) and wouldn't listen to the brothers (again).

The Plague of Gnats

The next trick in the repertoire is gnats. Or midges, or mosquitoes, or whatever you call them in your part of the world. Small, bitey flying bastards for wont of a better description. So, *"the LORD tells Moses, 'Tell Aaron to take your staff and strike the dust of the ground,' and throughout the land of Egypt the dust will become gnats"* (Ex. 8:16). Which he did, of course, and then there were gnats everywhere, biting people and animals and generally making life a misery for everyone and everything. Here's where we take a deviation from the usual, because, *"when the magicians tried to produce gnats by their secret arts, they could not"* (Ex. 8:18). And who could blame them, really? Who in their right mind would want to produce a great swarm of gnats? So, they told the pharaoh that since the buggers were everywhere, this was the *"finger of God"* (Ex. 8:19), but the Pharaoh was not listening and wouldn't let the peeps go.

So, gnats. Or midges, or mosquitoes. Same dog, different leg action. Why were there suddenly lots of them? Well, we have the waters of the Nile still clogged with red algal blooms and essentially being a large swamp until the rains returned to flush the river system of its toxic contents; but in the meantime it just happens to be a perfect breeding ground for – you guessed it – gnats. And because all the fish in the river had died through lack of oxygen in the water, there were no natural predators for the eggs, creating a huge imbalance in nature's life cycle and allowing most, if not all, of the eggs to reach maturity, resulting in the gnat plague. It's not that hard to logically account for the order of these plagues, at least thusfar. Let's continue and see what comes next, yes? Yes. Huzzah!

The Plague of Flies

God pisses in Moses' ear again, telling him to get up early and get in Pharaoh's face by the river, and tell him yet again to let the people go (Ex. 8:20). And that if he doesn't, he will, *"send swarms of flies on you and your officials, on your people and into your houses"* (Ex. 8:21). Further to that: *"On that day I will deal differently with the land of Goshen, where my people live; no swarms of flies will be there"* (Ex. 8:22). So apparently this all happened, and Egypt was rife with flies (Ex. 8:24).

Looking back, it's not really difficult to see why there was suddenly a fly plague. Thousands of frogs decomposing in the hot sun is a perfect breeding ground for flies, is it not? And with an abundance of food for maggots which then turn into flies, it's really quite understandable how this occurred by natural means. As for Goshen being fly free? A person with their weather-eye active could easily determine that the wind will be easterly on a given day, instead of the more usual westerly direction, thereby blowing the stink of dead frogs (and more importantly, the flies) in the direction of the Egyptians, leaving Goshen relatively fly-free.

No mention of the magicians this time around (perhaps they've all been sacked and/or put on a spike), but the Pharaoh summons the brothers and tells them to, *"Go, sacrifice to your God here in the land"* (Ex. 8:25). Moses counters by saying that this wouldn't be right, that the sacrifices are *"detestable to the Egyptians,"* and that if they did that, *"would the Egyptians not stone us?"* He suggests that he must journey three days away to do it. The Pharaoh permits this, but says, *"Don't go too far,"* like a bad cop warning a murder suspect not to skip town. Moses replies that he will head off and pray to remove the fly plague but warns the Pharaoh that he'd better not renege on this promise of letting the people go this time. Moses heads off, does his wailing, and the flies are gone by next morning (Ex. 8:26 – 8:30). As usual, though, the Pharaoh reneges and refuses to let the peeps go (Ex. 8:31).

So how do we explain the appearance and disappearance of the flies? Well, there are some species of fly (such as the Mayfly) that only live for twenty-four hours, which could explain this adequately. Although they are not attracted to decomposing frogs, they *do* feed on algae which the Nile currently has in plentiful supply. While I am not up to speed on all the species of flies in Egypt in biblical times, this explanation seems the most rational in terms of flies just appearing and vanishing almost as quickly. One could also argue that the winds changed again by the next day, blowing the flies towards Goshen to annoy them for a while. And while there is no record of that happening, I wouldn't put it past whoever wrote the bible to just omit that little snippet because it detracts from the story and makes God look like a limp noodle. Which, to be honest, he's achieving quite well off his own bat without any help from the author. Another explanation is that the Egyptians got sick of smelling like rotting frog, got themselves together and buried the bloody things under the desert sands, desiccating them utterly and removing a food source for more common flies and scavengers; but again, no mention of this occurring in the texts, so we can only speculate and hope for the best.

Exodus 9: Livestock and Boils and Hail, Oh My…! (and a hug for comfort)

"I sort of knew I was a bit of a drama queen. I always threw tantrums, so I knew I wasn't a normal child." -Millie Bobby Brown

Next on the list of plagues we have to play with is the Plague of Livestock. Now, although you might get an image in your head of Egyptians fleeing in terror from thousands of suddenly-appearing livestock in a grisly parody of the Running of the Bulls, you can relax because it's only that the livestock died, apparently. God tells Moses to get in the Pharaoh's face with the "Let My People Go" thing again; and this time he will, *"bring a terrible plague on your livestock in the field – on your horses, donkeys and camels and on your cattle, sheep and goats"* (Ex. 9:3). But once again, making a distinction between Egyptian and Hebrew livestock so that no Israelite livestock will die. And so, he did his hocus-pocus and the next day the Egyptian animals were plagued and dying while the Hebe ones were not. The Pharaoh for his part went out for himself and saw this for himself, but was as yet unyielding and refused to let the peeps go (Ex. 9:4 – 9:7).

A plague on livestock is also pretty simple to explain away, particularly when we think of the previous plagues of gnats and flies. Whilst the Egyptian people could counter the plagues by the simple expedient of swatting them, closing their doors or other such physical measures, the same could not be said for their livestock. With only tails to swish about their arses, this left a significant portion of animal exposed to insect attack; and with any such extreme attack from a plague of gnats and flies, it brings with it the passing on of blood-borne diseases to which an animal would quickly succumb. Again, a perfectly natural explanation to account for the plague of livestock, and all the other plagues, happening in a perfect chain of events that could have been foreseen by anyone willing to put a modicum of thought put into the matter.

The Plague of Boils

Now we're treated to God telling the brothers to, *"take handfuls of soot from a furnace and have Moses toss it into the air in the presence of Pharaoh. It will become a fine dust over the whole land of Egypt, and festering boils will break out on people and animals throughout the land"* (Ex. 9:8 – 9:9). So they did that, and the boils broke out, and everyone was covered in boils, hooray. The magicians (hey, they're back!) *"could not stand before Moses because of the boils that were on them and on all the Egyptians"* (Ex. 9:11), and once more *"the LORD hardened the Pharaoh's heart"* (bloody thing must be a diamond by now) and wouldn't listen to the brothers.

As we discussed with the livestock plague, the boils are simply a surface condition caused by all the infected insect bites. Antibodies to the most common diseases start doing their work and try to fight off the infection, resulting in nasty pus-filled boils erupting from the bites sustained by people and animals alike; which, while painful, are under normal circumstances harmless enough, if somewhat disfiguring in the short term. Certainly nothing mysterious in where they have come from or why, but if you were there at the time and all these things were going down, you could be forgiven for thinking some supernatural agent was running amok, particularly if you're the hard-of-thinking, goat-herding type.

The Plague of Hail

I do rather like this one, I have to admit. Moses gets told to front up the Pharaoh again and tells him to Let the Peeps Go yet again, *"or this time I will send the full force of my plagues against you and against your officials and your people, so you may know there is no one like me in all the earth"* (Ex. 9:14). He goes on to say that, ooh, I could have just struck you with a plague that would have wiped you off the earth, but that they were there for one purpose, to see the power of God and blah blah blah, so therefore on the morrow there will be a plague of hail such that Egypt has never seen, and all because the

Pharaoh won't let the people go (Ex. 9:15 – 9:17).

Now, readers of my last book will recall at this point my observations following Noah's Ark in that, despite God giving his pinky-swear not to drown everyone ever again, he still had some elements to play with, such as fire, earth, wind and disease. Now you could technically argue that hail is a *kind* of water, just colder and much harder and more inclined to kill you should you happen to get caught in a plague of it. You could think of it as God's way of stoning you to death without having to hold rocks up in the air with blatant disregard to Gravity and Physics. Anyway, he goes on to tell everyone to get their animals to shelter before the hail-plague, as any person or animal caught in it will die (Ex. 9:19). Those who were fearful of course brought their animals in, and those who weren't, didn't. And eventually Moses did his raise-the-hands-to-the-sky thing and the hail fell and did its hard, grisly thing.

Again, this can be explained by savvy watching of the skies. I recall early in my career, we were stopped at a station called Beete, which is about forty kilometres north of the nearest town of Salmon Gums. There had been thunderstorms and rain all that week, and the phones we used to communicate with the train controller were dropping in and out. I was getting a train order, and the controller at the time wanted to make it out to Beete; I reminded him of the telephone situation and suggested making the order to Salmon Gums instead, on the basis that if the station's phones were down, we could simply walk across to the pub a mere hundred yards away and get a further order from there. But no; "Proceed to Beete" was the order of the day. Sure enough, we dragged the train to Beete and wouldn't you know it, the phones were down.

After some spectacular language in which the controller's intelligence, appearance, wisdom and parentage were strongly questioned, the driver remained with the train while I was left facing a forty-kilometre hike back to Salmon Gums to procure another train order (lucky for me, the main road ran alongside the track, and I was able to secure a ride back to town). I got to the pub, received another train order, and then headed to the service station in hope of hitching another ride back to the train. Back then we had eight hour shifts, and walking eighty kilometres in that timeframe was out of the question (if you want to get a better perspective of that, set your treadmill at the gym to 10km/h, and then run on it for eight solid hours; go on, I actually dare you. Who says train drivers are lazy..?!).

On the way to the servo, I was looking at the very overcast sky, and it was unlike anything I have ever seen before, or since: it was almost as if someone had thrown a large grey blow-up mattress over the sky. The clouds were lumpy, in regular, round lumps, not entirely unlike a sheet of bubble-wrap hovering overhead; and I remember thinking, "That's not promising..!" I managed to find a lift back to the train, and on the way back, didn't it *hail!!* It was so heavy we couldn't see anything beyond the bonnet of the car, and it was all the driver could do to find the road, let alone get off it and under the dubious shelter of a tree; a brave choice when you consider that road shoulders in Australia turn to mud in weather that harsh. Anyway, we managed to get back to the train, and the trip continued. The point of the story is that, for the savvy weather-watcher, it's feasible to spot a bad weather front approaching and "predict" a hailstorm or large winds or whatever. Another unique characteristic of hailstorms is that, prior to their arrival, the sky will be alive with the sound of the hailstones bouncing off each other, sounding for all intents and purposes like one continuous roll of thunder. An ominous sound to hear if you're just a lowly goat herder with a limited grasp of meteorology, I would imagine.

Okay, where were we? Right, the plague of hail. Thousands of balls of ice, lurching zombie-like into the streets of Egypt, grinding against each other with hideous and glacial ominousness, and crushing any hapless Egyptians too slow to escape into a thin red paste. Well, perhaps not, but I do love a mental picture..! Anyway, trees were stripped of their leaves, sown crops were destroyed, and people and animals caught out in the storm were effectively stoned to death; or if they were lucky they were struck by lightning that was flashing back and forth as well, as we know that the friction caused by the collisions of hail and high winds generates a huge electric charge that regularly discharges in the form of lightning. The Pharaoh, of course, knew not of these things, leaving such matters to his court magicians, and thought he'd pushed his luck too far this time, summoning the brothers and confessing to them, *"This time I have sinned. The LORD is in the right, and I and my people are in the wrong"* (Ex. 9:27). He then implores the brothers to wail to their God to stop the hail, which they do; and when it stops, the Pharaoh again hardens his heart and refuses to let the peeps go (Ex. 9:29 – 9:35).

There's not much to add here. We are already aware that Pharaoh is being a prick and God is taking the credit for it, so nothing has changed since Moses hoofed it from the mountain, with the possible exception of God getting a kick out of screwing with humanity once again. Let's get moving with the next chapter and see what we can interpret from what remains of this drawn-out drama.

Exodus 10: Locusts and The Dark

"Education is the movement from darkness to light."
-Allan Bloom

We start this chapter with God telling Moses to front the Pharaoh yet again, to relay yet another message along the lines of, *"How long will you refuse to humble yourself before me? Let my people go, so that they may worship me;"* going on to say that his continued refusal would see locusts covering everything and eating what was not destroyed by the hail plague (Ex.10:3- 10:6).

After the brothers had left, the Pharaoh's staff expressed their frustrations, asking the Pharaoh to let the bloody people go already, and didn't he realize that Egypt was ruined? Hearing this, the Pharaoh dragged the brothers back before him and told them to go and pray or whatever but demanded to know who would be going to do this. Moses answered that it would be pretty much everyone and everything Hebrew; male and female, young and old, livestock and et cetera.

The Pharaoh was a little pissed at this, and said, *"If I let you go, with your women and children, you are clearly bent on evil! NO! Have only the men go and worship, since that's what you've been asking for"* (Ex. 10:10 – 10:11) before kicking the pair to the proverbial kerb. Moses didn't take that well, so after being told by God to wave his magic stick again, he held it aloft and, *"the LORD made an east wind begin to blow across the land"* which by morning brought the locusts into Egypt, where they began to consume all in their path (Ex.10:13 – 10:15). The Pharaoh pissed himself again and re-summoned the pair, said he had sinned, and begged them to get rid of the locust plague. Which, of course, Moses did, with his handy-dandy … God Stick, *DING!!* … right..!; creating a west wind which blew the locusts away. Which then re-hardened the Pharaoh's heart and he once again back-flipped like an Australian politician and refused, once more, to let the peeps go (Ex. 10:16 – 10:20).

Okay, so if we take all the previous plagues into consideration – the river algae and the frogs and gnats and flies and so on – locusts would also be fairly easy to explain. We have already discussed with the flies the feasibility of wind direction in the selective suffering of a country, and the locusts are no different. We are seeing a seasonal period of the year where the winds are variable from one direction to the next, as a result of high-pressure systems floating across the land mass as we all know from watching any television weather report, ever. Locusts, as we know, are highly migratory, requiring a lot of nutrient to maintain the swarm. Indeed, your typical locust swarm can cover up to 460 square miles of land (with between 40 million and 80 million insects in every half a square mile) and consume 423 million pounds of plant matter in a single day. With this much demand for food, the locusts must be constantly on the move to ensure the survival of the swarm. So of course, once the area they are in has been utterly eaten away, they will fly off, following the winds to preserve energy more than anything else, to find themselves in Egypt at this time. As Egypt has already been hit with other ecological events, it wouldn't take long for the swarm to eat what is left of the foodstuffs available before flying out again on the next available wind. A nice, short plague that, while brief, doesn't do anything to improve the situation for the poor Egyptians. Done is done, as they say, so let's see what this mad God has in store for them next.

The Plague of Darkness

As with our previous mental image concerning the Plague of Hail, I'm unsure how you could rightly classify Darkness as a "plague," but hey, let your imagination run wild with that while I lay down the premise of the story. After Moses got stiffed yet again by the Pharaoh's hardened heart, he hoists his hand to the sky (not his God Stick™ this time) and, *"total darkness covered all Egypt for three days. No one could see anyone else or move about for three days. Yet the Israelites had light in the places where they lived"* (Ex. 10:22 - 10:23). The Pharaoh summoned the brothers, permitting the women and children to go with the men, yet insisting the livestock remain behind (Ex. 10:24). Moses demurred, saying that they needed the animals for their offerings and sacrifices and that the livestock had to go as well (Ex. 10:25 – 10:26). The Pharaoh then finally lost all patience with Moses, and told him to, *"Get out of my sight! Make sure you do not appear before me again! The day you see my face is the day you die"* (Ex. 10:28). Moses for his part calmly and eloquently says (with that feeble tongue and mind of his), *"Just as you say, I will never appear before you again"* (Ex. 10:29).

Okay, let's get a couple of things into some sort of logical perspective here. Moses covers ALL of Egypt in darkness for three days. Well, the most obvious thing to explain this would be a solar eclipse; but as we know, solar eclipses last on average about two to three minutes tops, in their period of totality. It could well be possible that the original translator of the bible misread the thing (bearing in mind that the original texts would have been in Ancient Hebrew or some other dead language) and simply misread minutes as days.

Furthermore, we know that the area of totality covered by a solar eclipse is exceedingly small compared to the earth's surface. It is like an inverse example of a magnifying glass being brought into focus on an ant nest, except that instead of focusing the sun's rays, the moon's gravity slightly bends the rays and shrinks its shadow into a conical shape, and its distance from the earth makes the area of totality on the earth's surface to be roughly 110 kilometres in diameter. And considering that it's about 160 kilometres from Cairo to the Mediterranean, anyone observing the totality from Egypt would think the whole world had gone dark. Mind you, this is not allowing for the fact that the moon was closer to the earth at that time, albeit only slightly. Currently our moon is moving away from the earth at approximately 3.8 centimetres every year, so if we turn the clock back a few thousand years – the year 2018 minus the 1473BCE these events were supposed to have occurred – gives us $3491 * 3.8cm = 132.65$ metres closer to the earth back in Moses' time. In real terms, it only affects the diameter of the moon's shadow on the earth by about two kilometres at best and doesn't really have any discernable impact on the average goat-herding observer.

What *would* have an impact is the individual interpretation of the actual time elapsed during the event. I am reminded of an amusing axiom here: How long a minute is depends on what side of the bathroom door you're on. And we've all been there, haven't we readers? You're busting to use the facilities and you race to the only bathroom in the house, to find that someone else has beaten you to it, and you spend what seems an eternity pounding with biological desperation on the door until the guilty party finishes up. And of course, you have the opposite end of the spectrum, where you have beaten everyone else to the bathroom only to be instantly hounded with muffled pleas to HURRY UP FOR F*@#$'s SAKE!!! Time is, if nothing else, relative to the observer. I did ponder this very conundrum years ago, and I concluded with some amusement that your everyday household bathroom is, in fact, a black hole of sorts with its very own event horizon, represented physically as the Door. To expand the physics: in any given bathroom there are at least two, if not three, sink holes: Shower/bath obviously, the basin sinkhole (two if you're a yuppie!) and of course a toilet, the usage of any of which creates whirlpools in the water they collectively drain from the bath/basin/toilet respectively. And just like the black holes you might find in space, they warp the fabric of space and time, such that time slows as soon as you cross that event horizon (the bathroom door); so that to the outside observer who is at risk of a ruptured bladder, the person inside seems to have been inside the bathroom/black hole literally *forever*; whereas the person inside the event horizon, being unaware that they are caught in the temporal physics of black-holedom, have barely been in the room before they're accosted to leave it. I found it quite elegant actually, and while I don't expect any of you to believe my Bathroom Hypothesis for even one minute, I do feel it metaphorically explains much about the crazy universe in which we live!

Anyway, back to the darkness thing; let us for the sake argument apply some common-sense logic to the claims here. We are told in Ex. 10:22 that the darkness was total, and that *"no one could see anyone else or move about for three days, yet the Israelites had light in the places they lived."* Assuming this to be true, the darkness was obviously not *total* darkness; and if it was, and nobody could see anyone else or move around, how then did they perceive the light enjoyed by the Israelites? Further to this: The Pharaoh summoned the brothers to issue his decree. How was that achieved when nobody could see anyone else, nor move about the city? Someone is obviously lying here, or greatly exaggerating. While solar eclipses are renowned for turning day into night, it is never so dark as to prevent people from moving about and doing things and seeing people as if it was any other night of the week. Again, we should err on the side of the observers being awestruck by a total eclipse of the sun and being so frightened by it that their perception of time became elongated, as was their perception of how dark it really was. In a country full of sand and brightness, you could almost understand their perception of an event such as this. And while solar eclipses can occur up to twice a year, total eclipses are only visible on less than half a percent of the earth's surface; and then, you have to factor in planet rotation to determine exactly where the totality will occur (i.e. on land or sea), the time of year and so forth. So, a given geographical area may only experience a totality once in a hundred years or so, while some other regions may enjoy more of them on average. As it always is with real estate, it's location, location, location.

A last more extraterrestrial explanation could explain the darkness if we are required to stick to the three full days of darkness claim in the bible: Team Leader Yaweh established a geosynchronous orbit, ensuring the shadow of his ship remained over Egypt and obscured the sun from view for the time allotted. This in and of itself, however, brings its own subset of Size and Distance issues: To effectively block the sun over all of Egypt, an area spanning some one million square kilometres, God's ship would have to be equally large to effectively hide the sun completely; and even then, it would have to have a sufficiently low orbit to preclude penumbral areas around the shadow, which means the ship would be visible to people on the ground. Even a ship such as the iconic USS Enterprise (NCC-1701-D) is recorded in the Technical Manual as being 1,541 feet at its widest point (the saucer section); the shadow it would cast would be no bigger than

0.16 square kilometres, woefully short of the 1 million square kilometres it would need to cover. Indeed, the ship would have to rival that of the Harvester ship as seen in the second Independence Day movie, which the film claims to be the same diameter as Juptier's moon Europa (4,830km compared to our moon's slightly smaller 3,474km).

The other possibility is some form of solar sail dragged behind the ship, much like the sails proposed to propel spaceships using the solar wind; then at the appropriate time, Moses could just talk into the Stick of God, and the communications circuit inside would relay the instruction for the solar shade to be deployed. Perhaps; as unlikely as this last scenario would be, and the massive amount of effort going into the endeavour for minimal return, I include it only for the sake of covering all the bases.

Finally, the giggle-worthy exclamation of the Pharaoh to Moses to, *"Get out of my sight!"* (Ex. 10:28). Well, if the darkness plague means you can't see anyone else anyway (10:22), consider that order already fulfilled!

Exodus 11: The Plague on the Firstborn

"Even very young children need to be informed about dying. Explain the concept of death very carefully to your child. This will make threatening him with it much more effective." -P.J. O'Rourke.

Okey dokey, the first-born plague, huzzah! More death and misery doled out by the loving God of the Hebrews. Bring it on! We start this chapter as we have all the chapters relating to plagues, with God pissing in Moses' ear again and saying, *"I will bring one more plague on Pharaoh and on Egypt. After that, he will let you go from here and when he does, he will drive you out completely"* (Ex. 11:1). Okay, good; one more bit of unpleasantness, then it'll be smooth sailing for the Israelites. Nice.

God then tells Moses, *"Tell the people that men and women alike are to ask their neighbours for articles of silver and gold"* (Ex. 11:2). Okay, great, we're aware of this bit way back in Ex. 3:21 and the great plundering of the Egyptian people. So that wasn't entirely unexpected.

What we do not expect to see at this stage, is the following: *"(the LORD made the Egyptians favourably disposed toward the people, and Moses himself was highly regarded in Egypt by Pharaoh's officials and by the people.)"* (Ex. 11:3). I wouldn't exactly call it, "favourably disposed" but rather, "shit scared." Some old bugger with a stick sauntering around town performing acts of destruction and making others' lives a misery does *not* make him "favourably disposed" to anyone, unless you think extortion is a perfectly acceptable way to win friends and influence people. He's certainly no friend of the Pharaoh, who wants to rip off his head and put it on a sharp stick. If anything, the Egyptians would probably like nothing better than to be rid of the lot of 'em and to pick up the pieces of their shattered lives, thanks to those damnable slaves and their Bush God. So, if any exchange of gold and silver occurred, it was probably along these lines that they were able to procure such items of value, by robbing the Egyptians blind (Side Note: why they didn't just perform this theft during the Plague of Darkness is unclear, when the Israelites could see and the Egyptians could not. A discussion for another time, perhaps).

Anyway, Moses then states, *"This is what the LORD says: About midnight I will go throughout Egypt. Every firstborn son in Egypt will die, from the firstborn son of Pharaoh, who sits on the throne, to the firstborn son of the female slave, who is at her hand mill, and all the firstborn of the cattle as well"* (Ex. 11:4 – 11:5). There's some more stuff about much wailing and gnashing of teeth, and the Hebrew dogs not barking to mark some holy distinction between Israelite and Egyptian fortunes, and the Pharaoh's officials bowing to Moses and letting him go, et cetera; and then, *"hot with anger,"* Moses leaves the Pharaoh's presence. Another reference to God making the Pharaoh's heart hard to multiply his "miracles" and not letting the peeps go, aaaand end of chapter.

The real question is, who is this "I" that will go throughout Egypt? Is Moses referring to God, or himself? If it is Moses, it won't improve his popular standing with the people to have him running amok killing every firstborn child and animal in the countryside; and having Moses' mad God do the deed wouldn't be much better. It's once again mirroring the Saw movies, with God reprising the role of Jigsaw, callously and cruelly seeing just how far people will go before they snap, purely for his own sick and twisted amusement.

On a more logical footing now, the plague of the firstborn can be rationalized by human survivalist behaviours. With any family unit in ancient times, the firstborn child was obviously the most important member of the family besides the patriarch, often ahead of the wife and mother as was the standing of women back then. We've had a long string of "plagues" that have brought wrack and ruin to the area, and as a result any food that was available after that was going to be fed to the firstborn to ensure its survival. Now, considering we've had a plague of livestock where the animals have died from disease due to gnat and fly bites, and other plagues that have wiped out all other foodstuffs in the area, it's not unreasonable to assume that they have begun consuming the only remaining source of food: the flesh of the dead animals. It's not much of a stretch to imagine what will happen to these hapless firstborn children, now is it? And because the food shortage affected the city in its entirety, it's reasonable to say that people succumbed to the food poisoning at the same general time, allowing for gestation of the meat and the incubation time for the toxins to ravage the body. It completes a very grisly cycle in what could be considered a perfect storm of misfortune for the Egyptian people, with each step feeding off and leading to the next, with the inevitable end result. And if you've got a batshit-crazy Hebrew running around with a magic stick telling simple-minded people that a mad, vengeful god is going to come and knock off your first-born kid – and that kid begins to develop nausea, vomiting, fever, palpitations and so on – it's not hard to see how peoples' minds can be distorted by an alternative reality. This is why religious cults are such a Bad, Bad Thing.

Exodus 12: Of Lamb Roasts and Gluten Intolerance

"Passover is my idea of a perfect holiday. Dear God, when you're handing out plagues of darkness, locusts, hail, boils, flies, lice, frogs, and cattle murrain, and turning the Nile to blood and smiting the firstborn, give me a pass. And tell me when it's over." -P.J. O'Rourke

We launch into this chapter with God bailing up Aaron and Moses, who are still in Egypt, and telling them that *"this month will be the first month in your year"* (Ex. 12:2). So, we have some establishment of the Hebrew New Year, as vague as that is in relation to the Gregorian calendar we love today. God then says that, *"On the tenth day each man is to take a lamb for his family, one for each household,"* going on to explain sharing between small families on a one-between-two basis and general instructions on portion sizes and people to be served. The animals are, of course, to be without defect (can't be having any muties in there, especially after that Sodom incident!) and keeping the animals for four days, when at twilight they were to be slaughtered (Ex. 12:5). After their slaughter, they were to smear some of the blood all over the doorframes of the building they were going to eat the animal in, insisting that they animal be roasted with bitter herbs and bread made without yeast (Ex. 12:8).

So far, so good. Getting a sheep and watching it for four days to make sure it's not sick is a pretty good idea anyway. The thing about the bread made without yeast is mildly amusing, though. While scholars have decided that the order of yeastless bread was as a result of the Israelites' need to leave in a hurry and having no time to wait for the bread they were baking to rise, I rather fancy it was because God had some kind of gluten intolerance that gave him some righteous abdominal cramps. Or maybe it was just Moses that had the intolerance, and he decided that the best way to never have to eat gluten again was to say that God commanded it to be so. Whatever the reason, they now have to have flat, hard bread instead of the nice fluffy stuff we enjoy today.

As far as the blood on the doorframes are concerned, perhaps this is a tip-of-the-hat back to that nasty encounter back at the roadside where God wanted to kill Moses and his son got the impromptu bob-job. The red all over the doorframe could be a grisly parody of that particular slice-and-dice which kept the very unstable (and squeamish) God away from the homes of the Hebrews. Amazingly enough, I found an obscure reference to this very thing in the *Encyclopedia of Vernacular Architecture in the World (1997)*; where, in certain cultures such as the Dogon peoples of Mali (Africa), the house is perceived as part (or parts of) the human body.

The amazing coincidence for our particular story is that the front room of a house is usually considered to belong to the owner, or male partner of the family, and the front door represents – you guessed it – his genitals. Now, if you were to spread blood all around the door frame, what immediately springs to mind here? Occam's Razor (or perhaps it was Crazy Old Abe's Razor) would suggest this is amazingly coincidental for the casual observer, far more so to put it down to mere Serendipity.

Getting back to God's myriad culinary orders of roasting the lamb, eating the whole lot of it and burning what hasn't been eaten the next day, he also dictates how to eat this dubious fare. *"This is how you are to eat it: with your cloak tucked into your belt, your sandals on your feet and your staff in your hand. Eat it in haste – it is the LORD's Passover"* (Ex. 12:11). An amusing mental image to be sure, almost like Abe Simpson's rambling diatribe about wearing a brown onion on your belt, "because that was the style at the time." The actual reason is sadly just a practical one, to eliminate tripping over the bloody thing when you're running away from angry Egyptian sword points. Another reference is made to the blood on the door and God's reluctance to go anywhere near it – he must *really* be grossed out by foreskins despite, allegedly, creating them in the first place – before getting back to the yeast thing and commanding the Hebrews to not eat any bread with yeast in it for seven days. Additionally, they were to, *"remove the yeast from your houses, for whoever eats anything with yeast in it from the first day through the seventh must be cut off from Israel"* (Ex. 12:15). It seems a little ridiculous on the surface, but as with any weird instruction I find in this mad book, a dive into Google's Information Dumpster has turned up some interesting medical studies that show a direct relation between certain yeasts (such as Brewers Yeast) and the increased production of lactic acid in the body. Without the benefit of being a dietician, it is feasible to suppose that God is getting his peeps ready for the Red Sea Marathon: by eliminating yeast products from their diet for a week, it's possible that they will be able to run for a greater length of time before succumbing to lactic acidosis and, soon after, Egyptian swords. Just another hoop for this "Chosen People" to jump through, rather than just smiting the upstart Pharaoh with his finger and demanding exclusivity of worship.

Because, when you think about it, exactly how many gods do we have running about doing miracles and demanding worship and so forth? Furthermore, how has it come to pass that the alleged God of Creation has become so obscure a figure that the Egyptians don't recognize this god or, if they do, consider him a very minor one? Egypt at the height of its power had over two thousand gods, each one given an animal head to represent his or her particular power. These were a people who had a Top Ten list of favoured gods; Amun-Ra being the Head Honcho and then Mut, followed by Osiris, Anubis, Ra, Horus, Thoth and so on, each with their own unique responsibilities, powers and appetites. And then you have the gods of the foreigners such as the twelve Greek gods and eventually the twelve Roman gods (although they don't come into play here, at least not yet). If we refer to the Spaceman Scenario, could it be that Team Leader Yaweh, having washed his hands of the whole lot of Humanity (despite interfering at every single opportunity), was effectively sidelined by his crew, who were pissed off at being separated from the carnal delights of the "daughters of Men" and facing a life sentence of holographic porn to satisfy their biological urges? Deciding in fact to bugger him for a joke and create their own God-doms with the commensurate worshippers that resonate to the powers they claim to hold? It would explain how we went from one all-powerful god to a plethora of gods responsible for various things, especially if you consider that each member of a starship is ultimately responsible for a different ship function: engineering, science, exobiology, medicine, navigation, tactical, communication, astrophysics, military and so on. Each branch of the technological tree embodying a unique set of characteristics and behaviours that flesh out the new god and their appetites and failings. It is an elegant solution to the problem of getting many variegated gods from the one insanely jealous one, and one I happen to subscribe to the longer I run the path of logic through my head.

The issue of polytheism put gingerly aside for the moment, we'll return to our narrative, which was the eschewing of yeast-related foods because God hates cramps. He must be really intolerant, due to the command, *"For seven days no yeast is to be found in your houses. And anyone, whether foreign or native-born, who eats anything with yeast in it must be cut off from the community of Israel"* (Ex. 12:19). I think either extremely intolerant, or extremely jealous of anyone who can eat yeast and gluten with impunity, which doesn't say much about God's omnipotence if a yeast-laden falafel can bring the sucker down in a bloaty, crampy, flatulent ball of misery.

We next read about Moses gathering the elders and explaining to them the food things, and the dipping of hyssop (other than a "small bushy aromatic plant of the mint family," it's otherwise described as a, "wild shrub of uncertain identity used for ancient Jewish rites of purification") into blood for use as an ersatz paintbrush for their doorways, exhorting them that, *"None of you shall go out of the door of your house until morning"* (Ex. 12:22). A fair call, I say, if you have an insane god running amok in the streets after dark; losing your wallet and credit cards would be the least of your worries if you ran into that bundle of joy. Anyway, there are further rabbitings-on about telling your kids if (big IF) they ask in the future why they have to do this thing, and the reasons why, and blah blah blah. And then all the Israelites reported in as having done this thing; and then midnight rocked around, God went on his killing spree, and there was much wailing and gnashing of teeth, for, *"there was not a house without someone dead"* (Ex. 12:30).

Well, if that were true, then the blood smeared on the doorframe didn't do a shitload of good, now did it? The blood thing was supposed to help the occupants inside *avoid* the coming death; so how could every house contain death when promises were made to the contrary? Yes, yes, you could argue that it was only Egyptian houses, but why wasn't that distinction made, when pains were made to create distinctions in previous plagues? I have to admit that, while the constant stream of contradictions and sheer nonsense is a source of intense aggravation for me, it has given me an almost endless resource of material on which to write, and so I should at least be grateful for that small mercy, and enjoy that sun while it's still shining.

The Exodus (the actual one)

Okay, here we go! The thing we were building up to for the last eleven and a bit chapters, the Exodus! Chucky Heston is in his caravan now, warming up his Stick of God™ and getting his hair professionally streaked with grey, and practicing parting the waters in a small bucket the props crew have graciously provided. Yul Brenner has just opened the third packet of his five-pack-a-day habit and demanding more matches; and Yvonne De Carlo, her acting role complete now that Moses' son has had his bob job, has popped off to put her resume in for the female lead of The Munsters, a role with very disturbing parallels to this one.

We begin by Yul – oops, I mean, the Pharaoh – summoning Moses and Aaron (despite telling Moses he would die if he saw him again) and telling them, *"Up! Leave my people, you and the Israelites! Go and worship the LORD as you have requested. Take your flocks and herds as you have said, and go. And also bless me"* (Ex. 12:31 – 12:32). Insert a small chuckle from me as I consider the Pharaoh's words here: "GO! Sod off, the whole festering lot of you! Take your shit and GTFO already! Oh and also, bless me." As contrary as it is confusing, it's nonetheless in there, so we'll just have to run with it. The Egyptian populace are also urging the Israelites to leave, *"for otherwise, we will all die!"* (Ex. 12:33). The Hebes for their part took all the dough that had been made before it had a chance to be yeasted, and also extorted all the silver and gold items from the hapless Egyptians (Ex. 12:34 – 12:35). We are then told that *"the LORD made the Egyptians favourably disposed toward the people, and they gave them what they asked for"* (Ex. 12:36), but I would probably have used, "shit-scared of" in place of "favourably disposed toward." If you were in their place, and had a whole bunch of nasty shit happen to you in a short space of time, including the death of your eldest child, and then heard that it was the result of some pissed-off Hebrew god, you would probably hand over almost anything to be rid of them as well. As the adage says, "If you give someone five dollars and you never see them again, it was worth it."

We are told that the Israelite hoard – some six hundred thousand men on foot, plus women and children – journeyed from Rameses (the place, not the Pharaoh Ramesses) to Sukkoth, baking loaves of flatbread along the way. We are then told that, *"The dough was without yeast because they had been driven out of Egypt and did not have time to prepare food for themselves"* (Ex. 12:39).

Omfg no..! They had unyeasted dough because their batshit-crazy god told them not to have it! They had unyeasted dough because they were told they'd be cut off from their community if they were found in possession of it! They had at least four frickin' days, at the very least, to get their shit together prior to God's killing spree, so don't give me any of that, "didn't have time" rubbish! They had unyeasted bread because if God couldn't eat the stuff without suffering intestinally, then he'd be damned if anyone else could eat it. I could go on, but I believe I've made my point. Oh, and some minor retro-chronology where they claim that the Israelites were freed 430 years to the day that God promised them, well, 430 years ago. Pretty easy to do that with the benefit of hindsight; not so easy if you're doing it on the fly.

Passover Caveats

One small final passage for this chapter, which outlines the restrictions God put on his peeps in regards to the observance of Passover:

Firstly, no foreigner may eat it. Well, fine, we don't want your stupid food anyway;

Secondly, any slave you have bought may eat it, but only after you have circumcised him. Seriously?! I suppose that's the first instance of an eating place where they charge people by the head. Additionally, a temporary resident or hired worker can't eat it;

It has to be eaten inside, and none of the meat taken outside. And don't break any of the bones. As if that really makes a difference;

The whole community of Israel must celebrate it. Or else…. what?;

A residing foreigner who wishes to partake of Passover must have ALL of the males in his household circumcised, and no uncircumcised male may eat it. Refer to Rule Two re: charging per head for a meal. If I were the foreigner I would "pass" on the Passover, because it's not like you're going to get an appropriate refund to make up for a bad meal;

And finally, that the Passover laws apply to native and foreigner alike. Well, when in Rome, I suppose, but again, it's not like you're having to learn a new language or conform to their tax law; foreskins don't just grow back as a general rule of thumb.

So, we finally see the end of this protracted chapter. I suppose apologies are in order, but then there was quite a lot to cover in this part of our journey. Hell, they even made a movie out of it, so to dissect it in a fistful of pages isn't too bad. Of course, there are more adventures for Moses and his rag-tag band of fickle people, so take a deep breath, gird your loins (tuck those cloaks into your belts, guys!) and let's continue our own modern-day exodus.

Exodus 13: God Puts Dibs on the Kids, hates Donkeys

"Heck, what's a little extortion among friends? -Bill Watterson

First cab off the rank, God is telling Moses to, *"Consecrate to me every firstborn male. The first offspring of every womb among the Israelites belongs to me, whether human or animal"* (Ex. 13:1). Well, that was immediately contradictory; wanting every firstborn male, then immediately ignoring the distinction he made two seconds ago regarding gender (and, indeed, species). Hedging his bets, I'd wager. God then tells them all to commemorate this day as it's the day that they were freed from Egyptian slavery. Yaaaay. And immediately follows that with, *"Eat nothing containing yeast"* (Ex. 13:3).

The guy must really hate yeast; he bangs on about it for some time here, even to the point of banning it from the land itself (*"nor shall any yeast be seen anywhere within your borders,"* Ex. 13:7). Now we've all heard in our lives the tales of extreme peanut allergies, for example, and if an affected person even goes *near* a peanut they could die of anaphylaxis. It makes you wonder how they survived that long with such extreme reactions as this, but they somehow do. More to the point, how truly omnipotent is this God character that he cannot be around yeast and is afraid of foreskins? Did he not create both? If

91

on that day, the yeast he created almost killed him, would he not just be like, "Yeah, that shit ain't going anywhere near *my* creation," and then tossed it straight into his celestial recycle bin? The more we consider things like this, the more vulnerabilities we discover about this God guy, to the point that he's sounding less God-like with every chapter. If there was some event in our ancient past that suggested the presence of some powerful entity, then that power would have been technological rather than biological.

Let's see now: more stuff about consecrating first-born things, keeping the ordinance for year after year (basic anniversary stuff); that, once the land of the Canaanites is given over to them, they're to do the giving of the first-born to God again. Oh, here's an interesting one: *"Redeem with a lamb every firstborn donkey, but if you do not redeem it, break its neck"* (Ex. 13:13). What a senseless and pointless thing to do! What did the bloody donkey ever do to deserve such an ignoble death, other than be born? Maybe God was kicked by a donkey once and he just has it in for them, or simply preferring a lamb roast to a donkey for which he has no practical use; but then why sentence the thing to death because the owner didn't have some lamb on hand with which to redeem it? Why demand the handing-over of every firstborn thing, and then be like, "Naah, I don't really want the donkeys, but if you have a nice juicy lamb instead, we'll call it even-Stevens?" Ridiculous.

Crossing the Sea

A short little passage here to end Ex. 13, about the initial flight path. It is mentioned here that God, *"did not lead them on the road through the Philistine country, though that was shorter. For God said, 'If they face war, they may change their minds and return to Egypt.'"* (Ex. 13:17). Instead, he took them via the scenic route, via the Red Sea. Now immediately contradictory to that verse, it reads, *"The Israelites went up out of Egypt ready for battle"* (Ex. 13:18). Ooookay... if they were leaving Egypt "prepared for battle," then why would they change their minds when faced with that battle, whether it be against Egyptians or Philistines or whoever? Does God have so little faith in his chosen people that he thinks they'll cut-and-run at the first sign of battle, despite being ready for that battle AND having a god on their team? The phrase, "Ye of little faith" springs to mind here.

It goes on to say that Moses was lugging the bones of Joseph with him, because of an oath he had made the Israelites swear, not to leave him in Egypt; fair enough, whatever. So they left Sukkoth, and travelled to Etham where they set up camp. It is said that, *"the LORD went ahead of them in a pillar of cloud to guide them on their way* and by night in a pillar of fire, so they could travel by day or night," and that, "neither pillar ... left its place in front of the people" (Ex. 13:21 – 13:22). So, we have God physically there at the vanguard of his peeps, albeit with a cloudy/fiery pillar of protection. And how to account for these "pillars" of either cloud or fire? If we hold to the rationale that "God" was a being from an advanced civilization, we could deduce that the cloud was generated from a low-flying craft of some sort, kicking up the desert dust; while at night, the flames from the maneuvering jets would be much more visible and giving the illusion of a cloud of fire. Without actually being there at time, it is impossible to tell with any accuracy, but this reasoning fits as well as any other, and the physics is there to support it, at least. The practical and logical side of that endeavour, though, to have your scoutcraft of death hovering about burning fuel 24/7 in basic stationkeeping duties is pretty bloody stupid in anyone's opinion. And additionally, to do all of this just to screw about with humanity leads me to seriously question God's mentality on top of the inefficient use of finite resources. But we are only mortals being manipulated like pawns in a greater game, so we'll move on for now and see what fresh nonsense God has in store for our band of hapless Hebes.

Exodus 14: God Baulks the Pharaoh, Passes Water (Parts!! Parts Water!)

"It's a trap..!" -Admiral Ackbar

We begin this chapter with God telling Moses to tell the people to hoof it back toward some place called Pi Hahiroth, between Migdol and the sea, directly opposite Baal Zephon. The reasoning, we are told, is that the Pharaoh will see these errant course changes and think that the Israelites are wandering about in a state of confusion whilst being hemmed in by desert on all sides. God once again promises to "harden Pharaoh's heart" – that thing must be a bloody diamond by now – and encourage him to give chase to the refugee Hebrews (or refugeebrews, if you will; patent pending). He then bangs on about giving himself glory through the Pharaoh and his cronies, and then they'll all know he's the LORD, and blah, blah, blah (Ex. 14:3 – 14:4).

Then we read: *"When the King of Egypt was told that the people had fled, Pharaoh and his officials changed their minds about them and said, 'What have we done? We have let the Israelites go and have lost their services!'"* (Ex. 14:5). Well, yeah, you told them to go, dude; what slave in their right mind is going to hang around to be told twice? The Pharaoh flies into a panic and organizes, *"600 of the best chariots, along with all the other chariots of Egypt, with officers all over them"* (Ex. 14:7). So just how many chariots were there, exactly? And why would you even bother to distinguish between the 600 "best chariots" if you're just going to drag every other chariot in Egypt along with you? It sounds as if the writer of the story wanted to impress the reader with the thought of six hundred magnificent chariots charging in hot pursuit; then decided it wasn't enough and hastily included all the others ones that might've had cracked wheels or a missing spoke or two bringing up the rear like the fat asthmatic kid you remember in your gym class. Anyway, hard-hearted Pharaoh is in charge of all the chariots and he's charging headlong towards the refugeebrews (patent pending) and probably yelling something appropriate while the aforementioned were, *"marching out boldly"* (Ex. 14:8). Confidence, that's the ticket here: you might be confused and afraid and watching all the chariots of Egypt bearing down on you with murderous intent, but so long as you look like you're doing it with confidence, then it'll all work out okay. Probably. The author is almost certainly taking liberties and painting a picture of resolute bravado against overwhelming odds to attempt to sway reader sympathy. Can't say I blame him, I'm doing it myself. Anyway, the Egyptian horde pursued and overtook the refugeebrews as they camped by the sea at the previously mentioned Pi Hahiroth (Ex. 14:9).

It's a bit silly, really; if the Egyptians overtook the fleeing people, it would suggest that they were in fact apprehended, and ipso facto would have been frog-marched back to Egypt to pick up where they left off with their indentured servitude. Semantics, I suppose. Anyway, the people saw this Egyptian horde bearing down on them and promptly shat themselves (with admirable boldness, no doubt). They cried out to the LORD (Ex. 14:10), as if that was going to help. They turned to Moses and asked him why he brought them out into the desert to die, that they told him to leave them to their slavery in peace, that it would have been preferable to be a slave than to be a speed-hump for Egyptian chariots (Ex. 14:12). Moses, for his part, told the people not to be afraid, to stand firm, and *"see the deliverance the LORD will bring you today,"* and that, *"the LORD will fight for you; you need only be still"* (Ex. 14:13 – 14:14).

I would have loved to have seen the look on Moses face when God then said, *"Why are you crying out to me?"* That look of blank horror when he thought God was going to just sit back and throw him under the chariot in front of the people he promised to rescue. Pure gold! Sadly, however, he continues and tells him to get the Israelites moving; to use his magic stick to divide the water so that they can go through the sea on dry ground (Ex. 14:15 – 14:16). More guff about hardening hearts so they get chased into the gap in the water, more bragging about gaining glory through the Egyptians, claiming they'll then know who they're messing with, by cracky! Then God does the only useful thing so far in this saga, which is to interpose his cloud of dust to block the passage of the Egyptians, who have obviously not overtaken the refugees yet despite assurances from Ex. 14:9 that they had already.

So, with this dusty cloud barrier separating the armies (the refugeebrews are now an army, not a mere rag-tag group of fleeing slaves), Moses waves his arms about and, *"all that night the LORD drove the sea back with a strong east wind and turned it into dry land. The waters were divided, and the Israelites went through the sea on dry ground, with a wall of water on their right and on their left"* (Ex. 14:21 – 14:22).

Now to the physics. The place where this was supposed to have occurred, connecting Pi Hahiroth in Sinai with the west coast of Saudi Arabia, is generally considered to be about two thirds into the guts of the Gulf of Aqaba; the divided waters creating a roughly east-west path about nine miles long and about two hundred metres at its deepest point. So we're talking about a significant amount of water that needs to be retained by a mere easterly wind, regardless of strength and speed.

If you have a spa or jacuzzi at home, I strongly encourage you to try the following experiment. Grab/buy/borrow yourself a leaf blower and, aiming the nozzle at the water at one end of the spa, try to recreate a trench of dry land from one end of the spa to the other just by the wind power alone. It's much more fun if your spouse or significant other is standing at the other end of the spa monitoring your efforts!

Did we observe how the water interacted with the wind from the blower? Without some form of barrier to hold the water back, it simply collapses into the hole/depression/whatever you want to call it, replacing the water that was displaced by the wind erosion. We can sit there all day if we wanted to, with the only notable achievements being a drenched spouse and a slightly emptier jacuzzi. To be utterly blunt: the practical effect of a "strong wind" would *not* be dry ground as the bible suggests, but would be, at best, a perpetual water-slide effect of a speed that would make the most fearless adrenaline junkie shit himself. Your typical leaf blower generates a windspeed of about 280km/h at the nozzle, which quickly reduces as the force is mitigated by external forces such as prevailing winds, interaction with objects, loss of impetus, et cetera. If a channeled windspeed of 280km/h cannot even create a two-metre channel of any appreciable depth in a spa/jacuzzi, we can only imagine the windspeed required to create and maintain a channel *nine miles long and two hundred metres deep*. And even if such wind speeds were possible, anyone attempting to enter the channel would be rag-dolled across the rocky sea bed and expelled violently out the other side, launching the battered corpse with a force that would see it land somewhere in the vicinity of Kuwait.

If we instead entertain the possibility of "God" being a member of an advanced species visiting earth and lording it over the lesser ape-like hominids, we could argue that this channel of water was made possible with the use of force fields generated from … well, wherever. At our current state of technological development, we are unable to create any sort of physical barrier with nothing but thin air; but some day we may learn the trick of it, opening humanity to huge opportunities to explore our galaxy first-hand instead of from afar through our telescopes. But never mind that for now: with a pair of force fields running east-west and holding the water either side at bay, creating a trench of sorts, a focused wind *could* feasibly work.

Once the water was gone, the force fields would of course hold the water at bay keeping the trench dry, but I can only boggle at the sheer energy required to maintain not one, but *two* fields of that magnitude. At a depth of two hundred metres, the sea water is exerting a pressure no less than 2111.69 kPa, or 306 psi in the old measurements; or about twenty times atmospheric pressure (20.8 atm) at any given point of the barrier. To put that into better perspective, the total force exerted by the water on a barrier 9 miles long and 200 metres high would be:

$F = D*g* (h/2) * (w*h)$ where;

D = density of water (constant 100kg/m³)

g = gravitational acceleration (9.8m/sec²)

h = height of water/barrier

w = width of barrier

which gives us a Force of:

$100 * 9.80 *(200/2) * (30577.5*200)$

= 283,888,360 KiloNewtons of force acting on the shield/barrier/whatever. This is the equivalent of, say, 709,721 modern-day locomotives in their highest power notch, each pulling about 400KN, just to hold the barrier, let alone move it. Which isn't the case here, of course, but one problem at a time, yeah..?

Whether that is something that can be achieved with any sort of technology is anyone's guess, but we are a long way away from that point, that's for sure. At the very least, if it's possible for an advanced species to traverse the vast distances of space to reach our unremarkable rock, it would be equally capable of making a pedestrian trench in the water, if it felt like doing so.

Anyway, back to the narrative. The waters have parted, the path is made, and the refugeebrews are legging it to safety, into what is now Saudi Arabia, with the Egyptian army in hot pursuit (Ex. 14:23). God, for his part, looked from his fiery smoky pillar of whatever it was and threw the Egyptian army into confusion, and, *"jammed the wheels of their chariots so that they had difficulty driving"* (Ex. 14:25). So, was it another wave of the hand here, or did God decide to swoop down and jam some sticks into the spokes? And let's assume the chariots have spoked wheels, considering they've been around since their development by the Sintashta culture circa 2000 BC. Besides, it's an amusing mental image having God running about amongst a horde of over six hundred chariots and chucking sticks into the spokes. It rather fleshes out the idea of a batshit-crazy God, and to be perfectly honest I wouldn't put it past him to do just that.

At this stage, the Egyptians have lost their lust for blood and are crying, *"Let's get away from the Israelites! The LORD is fighting for them against Egypt"* (Ex. 14:25). So, they're starting to believe in this god of Hebrews, are they? Not "their" lord, but "the Lord", as if no other gods were floating about at the time. And we know that's not true at all because Egypt at the height of its civilization had over two thousand deities in its pantheon. It's pretty hard to imagine them all just sitting back idly, watching a new god run amok over their worshippers. You would think at least a few of them would team up and give this shithead god a royal arse-whooping. Horus God of Vengeance would be champing at the bit to get some payback, certainly; and Montu God of War would want in on that action, too. If we chuck in Amun-Ra as Supreme God Guy and the God-Most-Desperate-To-Maintain-His-Image-As-Superior-God, that's already a three-against-one contest, right there. So where were they for the Egyptian people? Even assuming they existed, such a non-interference status may explain why their worshipper numbers took a hit; but seriously, were they that self-absorbed that they couldn't band together and battle this one god and kick him to the astral kerb, so to speak? Talk about divine betrayal!

So yes, the Egyptians are all panicking and not getting support from their own gods and are trying to turn their recalcitrant chariots back out of the watery trench, but hampered in their efforts by the chariots at the back still trying to charge into the fray. Then God said to Moses, *"Stretch out your hand over the sea so that the waters may flow back over the Egyptians and their chariots and horsemen"* (Ex. 14:26). So he does that, and at daybreak (delayed effect, perhaps?) the sea went back into its place. And the water flowed back and covered the chariots and horsemen, and *"not one of them survived"* (Ex. 14:28).

A couple of things here. It would be hard to imagine the Pharaoh not being at the head of his army to crush these refugeebrews (patent pending) considering God had "hardened his heart" so many times during this saga it could probably shatter Adamantium. He would want Moses' head onna stick come hell or high water (shameless pun intended), and yet there is no mention in the history books of Ramesses II dying in his coronation year as a result of chasing some mad old Hebrew with a magic stick into a watery trench and being drowned. This is especially the case when you consider that Ramesses II died in 1213 BC at the age of ninety-one. You would think, at some stage of the history books, there would have been some passing mention of chasing a bunch of slaves between two walls of water, unless the defeat was placed firmly under, "Now Let Us Never Speak Of It Again On Pain Of Death." It's what I would have done in his place. Interestingly, however, a CT scan performed on the mummy of Ramesses II in 2014 allegedly found traces of sea salt. Coincidence? Well, probably not. Salt (or more precisely, Natron) was known to be a great preservative and desiccant and as such was used as part of the mummification process, and was typically harvested from dry lake beds at the time, so it's not really surprising to find it there. It was probably the result of a Creationist trying to find some divine meaning where none exists, perhaps claiming the sea salt found in the stomach indicated drowning ... a noble idea, were the internal organs not removed as part of the mummification. Eh, what can you do..?

As far as the water "flowing over" the hapless Egyptian army is concerned, I feel, "flowing" is perhaps the wrong word here. Imagine if you will these walls of water suddenly collapsing to fill the trench, each with a force of 283 million kiloNewtons, slamming shut on the Egyptian army like a wet book. It would be equivalent to having approximately 28,491,358 tonforce units (tf) dropped on you. For reference, one tonforce is the force exerted by the weight of one ton due to standard gravity.

That's over 28 million tonnes. From each wall. And you're the literal meat in that proverbial sandwich. There is no scenario where that is going to end well. Now, if a mere landmine in the Vietnam war could turn a soldier into what they referred to as, "goop" (essentially, the emulsification of the human body from the pressure of the blast), the sudden application of 28.4 million tonnes of pressure would have reduced the entire army to a thin red paste, their breastplates and other armour crushed to pancake-thickness with utter disregard to the flesh contained therein. To achieve such a complete violation of the human body would require it to be near ground zero of a nuclear detonation, if we were to try to draw a parallel with the modern era. Put bluntly, those poor bastards would not have known what hit them, which in and of itself is a blessing. If you gotta go, it's perhaps best to go so quickly that you don't even realize it until a dark hooded figure with a penchant for agricultural equipment is tapping your shoulder – which you feel purely out of habit – and beckoning you toward your next big adventure.

Okay, let's finish up the chapter. We next read, *"That day the LORD saved Israel from the hands of the Egyptians, and Israel saw the Egyptians lying dead on the shore"* (Ex. 14:30). Well okay, we've already covered that; there wouldn't be any dead Egyptians lying on the opposite shore after that much force was exerted on their persons, let alone the problem of seeing a shoreline nine miles away when the earth's curvature would obstruct your view beyond 4.7 miles; but in saying that, we have a new theory on why it is called the Red Sea. After all, the combined emulsification of so many men and horses would have given the water quite a haemoglobinny, not to mention syrupy, aspect. Mystery solved! Moving on.

When the Israelites see the carnage, they *"feared the LORD and put their trust in him and his servant Moses"* (Ex. 14:31). Understandable, that they would fear someone who has just crushed the entire Egyptian army into a thick, pink liquid. An excellent motivator, it must be said. And Moses, of course, gains a few Awe Points (AP), achieves Level 81, and wisely distributes his Skill Points towards Charisma and Strength, what with some more public speaking and the lugging of some stone tablets somewhere in his immediate future. And that's the end of that chapter.

Exodus 15: The Musical

"I hate musicals. There, I said it." -Aaron Paul

Oh dear God no, not singing. Anything but singing! Didn't we suffer enough when Frozen came out?!?! Have mercy, for pity's sake..!!!!!

Well, perhaps the wrong God to pray to when it comes to such concepts as Mercy, so we'll just have to suck it up. Apparently, Moses and the Israelites sang a song to the LORD. I won't go into detail on this; not only because we've already gone through the motions in the last chapter, but mostly because my singing talent is somewhere in the second percentile, nationally (which is slightly lower than a farting walrus). Suffice it to say that, being totes overwhelmed with Awe at all the Happenings That Cannot Be Fathomed With Primitive Minds, the natural response is to put it into Song. Later on, they'll chuck in a couple of Yeas and Verilys and then nobody will be able to refute the Truth of all the Things. Okay then.

Weeell, there is one part of the song I will refer to here before we move on: *"Who among the gods is like you, LORD?"* (Ex. 15:11). Who among the *gods*. Are we to read from this that God, by the bible's own words, has allowed (or created) other gods? The selfish, jealous, smitey God of Creation, creating other gods and sharing power, and as a result diminishing his own omnipotence?! I think not, dear readers! The

God of the Old Testament doesn't strike me as the type to tolerate competition. It just doesn't make sense! And how would you go about making a God anyway, even if you were a god yourself? As a font of absolute power, if he were to create another godlike being, the Law of Conservation of Energy would mean he would have to use that power to create the new god, diminishing himself significantly in the process. And there is no guarantee that this new god would see himself (or herself) as subservient, or even equal. They could easily see themselves as superior to the old god and attempt to usurp his place as Head Honcho. Nooo, I can't see this happening one little bit.

So what are we left with, this being the case? That gods are simply a creation of the human mind to explain things the primitive mind is incapable of understanding, nothing more. As we become more knowledgeable in the myriad fields of Science, we get closer to understanding the very nature of the Universe, and how things happen and why, and as a result we succumb less and less to baseless superstition and blind faith, and this can only be a Good Thing™.

The Waters of Marah and Elim

So now we have Moses leading the newly-freed refugeebrews away from the Red Sea and into the Desert of Shur, bumping along for three days without finding any water, which impressed his followers not a whit. They finally rocked up at a little place called Marah which had water, but they couldn't drink it because it was bitter (hence the name of Marah, a Hebrew name for "Place Wot Has Bitter Water We Can't Drink And Thanks For Nothing, Moses"). Naturally, they bitch and moan to Moses and complain about the lack of drinking water, so Moses, *"cried out to the LORD, and the LORD showed him a piece of wood. He threw it in the water, and the water became fit to drink"* (Ex. 15:25). Further, God *"issued a ruling and instruction for them and put them to the test."*

Sounds like a safety interaction to me, and pay attention because there'll be a test afterward, hardy-har-har. But firstly, the bit with the wood and the bitter water. We can safely assume that there will be some water in any given desert, and that not all of it will be drinkable, which depends on things like depth, warmth, mineral content, et cetera, and this Marah would be one such place. The bitter taste could be attributed to such things as dissolved metals in the water, such as iron, copper or galvanized pipes. Well, not galvanized pipes back then, obviously, but perhaps the first two. There may even be a few bacterial agents that could thrive in these sorts of conditions. But what, I hear you screaming ardently, is with the wood? Okay, okay, jeeze louise. Lovers of the website IFLScience may have seen an article regarding making water safe for drinking using a simple tree branch (for more details, search for, "simple tree branch filter makes dirty water drinkable" and be amazed). For those lacking the interweb, what we have found is that tree branches are very effective at filtering water. As we should all know from our time in school, plants and trees get their water and essential minerals through their root systems, and these nutrients get sucked up into the tree through Capillary Action. But furthermore, it turns out that any particles larger than 70 nanometres are filtered by the xylem (basically, porous tissue arranged in tubes) in the sapwood (the younger branches of any given tree) which includes any harmful bacteria that may be lurking in the water.

The practical upshot of all this Science-y stuff is that you can filter several litres of water per day with a relatively small piece of sapwood, not only eliminating the bitter taste but removing 99% of E. Coli from the water in the deal. Noice! And so, thanks to a little Knowledge, we can now rationally explain why we're putting wood into water to make it drinkable. Too much to expect from a primitive human society perhaps, but certainly not beyond a space-faring species of indeterminate origin.

God goes on to say that, if they pay attention to his commands and listen to his decrees, they wouldn't suffer any diseases or nastiness, because he was the LORD who heals them (Ex. 15:26). Totally a safety interaction. Listen to my instructions, do what I say, and you won't die horribly. All that's missing is the bloody sign-off sheet: here you go guys, put a scribble here to say you've understood the learning module, okay here's your drinking stick, off you go now. Ugh…

Oh, and then they got to Elim, which had twelve springs and seventy palm trees (like we care) and they camped near the water. As you would I suppose, being in a desert. I guess the tree and spring numbers will mean something at some stage, or perhaps not. Time will tell as it always does. Moving on.

Exodus 16: It's Raining Men... er, Bread..

"For he on honey-dew hath fed, and drunk the Milk of Paradise." -Samuel Taylor Coleridge

Later, the refugeebrews set out from Elim into the Desert of Sin. Nothing ominous about that, nosirree. Complete figment of the wossname. Thing you see non-existent things with, can be quite vivid. Religion! Er, I mean, Imagination! Anyway, they're in this desert and now they're bitching about how there's no food and, of course, blaming Moses for their ills: *"If only we'd died by the LORD'S hand in Egypt! There we sat and ate all the food we wanted, but you have brought us out into this desert to starve this entire assembly to death"* (Ex. 16:3). Bloody ingrates, only thinking about their own comforts and gains like a corrupt politician. It's a wonder Moses didn't just tell them all to bugger off; but then he was under the thrall of a god who doesn't tolerate "no" for an answer, and as such became the scapegoat for the ills of the Israelites.

Anyway, God comes to the rescue apparently, and says to Moses, *"I will rain down bread from heaven for you. The people are to go out and gather enough for that day. In this way I will test them and see whether they will follow my instructions"* (Ex. 16:4). He goes on to say that, on the sixth day, they're to gather twice as much as other days

(Ex. 16:5). Moses and Aaron then relay the instructions to the whingers.

So how to account for this weird description of "bread from heaven" beyond an image of God grabbing loaves out of his floaty cloud-oven and chucking them over the side for the pack of whiners below? Well, one explanation suggests that it was the sap of the Tamarisk (or Tamarix) tree. The basic theory is that various insects would process the pollen from these trees and excrete them as a sap on the ground overnight, resembling golden drops of dew. When the new day dawned and the rest of the normal dew evaporated, this sap-dew stuff would remain and was collected by the Israelites. It would, of course, require a huge amount of dew to sustain the needs of a crowd that large, some 603,550 men over the age of 20, according to Numbers 1:46; not to mention the women, the children, the livestock and so on, all of them wanting something to eat. But assuming this to be the case, it is interesting to note that this sap substance is also known as Honeydew. Once described by Samuel Taylor Coleridge as "the milk of paradise," the sap has a very high sugar concentration, which could at a pinch give the people the energy intake required to survive another day, perhaps. It really depends on how much insect excrement you're willing to eat on a daily basis.

So, now we have some vaguely plausible idea of how they survived in the desert, let's move on. We are told that Moses and Aaron, *"said to all the Israelites, 'In the evening you will know it was the LORD who brought you out of Egypt, and in the morning you will see the glory of the LORD, because he has heard your grumbling against him.'"* (Ex. 16:6). The two brothers personally relaying this message to some half-million Israelites, without the benefit of megaphones or public address systems or anything like that. Well, maybe they repurposed the odd goat horn or cupped their hands; but it would still take a bloody long time to personally pass the message on to that many people. Yes, they could well have delegated the message to their family or something, but anybody who's had to play Chinese Whispers in school knows how well that method of information dissemination works. Basically, the brothers are telling 'em to quit their bloody whining already, and their grumbling is actually against God, not them, as they're just following God's weird demands for them to wander the desert and go here and do that, et cetera, so don't come bitching to them about their woes. It's quite handy when you're able to fob off all your bad decisions onto some mysterious invisible entity, isn't it, although we are supposed to believe that God wasn't the neglectful, absent parent type we experience in today's world. No, back then he was more the violent, hands-on, mentally disturbed type you didn't want to annoy, or God help you (sad pun intended).

Knowing this penchant for smitey fiery death possessed by our god of choice, the brothers may have opted to disseminate the information themselves. But even there, and assuming they spoke to a hundred or so people each time and moving to the next group of whiners, there is a problem in that no two orations would be the same. If you've ever had to perform any public speaking, you will know that as you perform subsequent orations, you will unconsciously refine your technique; your manner will relax a little as you become more acquainted with your subject matter, you may substitute one word for a more fitting one, and so on. So, by the time you perform your last speech, it would be quite different to your first one. Perhaps this in itself can explain why we encounter so many splinter cults today. One group was told this, while the other group heard something slightly different that put a whole new spin on the message.

Even something as subtle as emphasis can alter the nature of the message entirely. If I said to you, "I want that toy dog," would you know what I meant by that?

Would you, though?

It's a simple five-word sentence, surely it can't be interpreted any differently to how you read it, right? But what if we change the emphasis on each word? Consider the following statements with the emphasized word highlighted and see how the meaning changes:

"*I* want that toy dog." *(and I'll fight you for it)*;
"I *want* that toy dog." *(but I can't afford it)*;
"I want *that* toy dog." *(and no other toy dog)*;
"I want that *toy* dog." *(and not a real dog)*;
"I want that toy *dog*." *(not the stupid toy cat)*.

Five words, five emphases, five very different meanings. It is the prime reason why posts on social media can go so incredibly pear-shaped and unintentionally offend a lot of people. But then, those people are usually looking for offence where none exists, and more often than not their mind fills in the blanks in the way they prefer, i.e. finding offence, giving them the permission they need to go apeshit on the hapless poster. So guys, if you encounter a post you don't like, pause a moment and consider the possibility you've misinterpreted the post. You're all bright, intelligent people (you're here reading my book, that's proof enough!) and a little bit of critical evaluation beforehand might save a lot of embarrassment later on.

Okay, moving on. Moses makes further promises to the mob along the lines of *"meat in the evening and bread in the morning"* (Ex. 16:12). We are then told, *"That evening quail came and covered the camp, and in the morning there was a layer of dew around the camp"* (Ex. 16:13). Well, we already know about the dew, so I won't elaborate any further on that unless something extra pops up; the quail, however, require some rationalization. We could, of course, amuse our respective sarcastic bents by imagining God up on his cloud tossing freshly-created quail over the side of his cloud along with the afore-mentioned bread; but a more prosaic answer would be that the flight patterns of the quail were already known to God (or Moses, who had already spent time in the area back from when he offed the Egyptian overseer) and as such either could have conned their way into that feat of soothsaying.

Quail are quite habitual in their feeding patterns, following an established route in their territory; so much so that they will appear at the same spot at almost the exactly the same time, every day of the year. When you add a steady supply of honeydew-secreting insects to the mix, it's not hard to see why the birds would do this. Ultimately, it's not really that hard to deduce that the refugeebrews were led to an area where a ready source of food was available. Mind you, six hundred thousand mouths plus women and livestock would have sorely tested even the most reliable of food reserves, a scenario not unlike a plague of locusts for the utter decimation of food in the area.

That's the quail explained. We then read on to find the Israelites confused about the thin flakes of frost left on the ground after the dew had evaporated, not knowing what it was. They were told, *"It is the bread the LORD has given you to eat"* (Ex. 16:15). Now, let us be perfectly clear about this: the all-seeing, all-powerful, all-wise, all-knowing God has given his Chosen People bug shit to eat. Actual bug shit. Yes, it's full of sugar, and Samuel Taylor Coleridge thought it was pretty good stuff, but then he also enjoyed laudanum on a more-than-casual basis. And it still comes out the arse end of an insect, when all is said and done. Given the choice, I think I would prefer to eat one of C.M.O.T. Dibbler's patented sausages inna bun than a hearty meal of divine bug shit, but I speak only for myself in this matter. And while we're addressing the elephant in the room, let's ask ourselves this: did the Israelites, or did they not, take their livestock with them when they fled Egypt on their exodus? Of course they did, we all read Ex. 12:31: *"Take your flocks and herds as you have said, and go (and also, bless me)."* So why the *fuck* would you want to eat bug shit when you have goats and sheep and cattle readily available for your consumption? Or did they just not take the time to think that through?

Anyway, back to the story. God is feeling very generous with his supply of bug shit because he commands everyone to, *"gather as much as they need. Take an omer (approx. 9.3 cups) for each person you have in your tent"* (Ex. 16:16). So they all did that and gathered all they wanted, some a lot, some a little (me, I'm still waiting for Dibbler to rock up). And when they measured it by the omer, *"the one who gathered much did not have too much, and the one who gathered little did not have too little. Everyone had gathered just as much as they needed"* (Ex. 16:18). So, either the omers in biblical times were open to individual interpretation, or it was stockpiled and doled out equally, or the story is complete bugshit. I know which option I'm leaning towards right now. Either way, everyone manages to score for themselves 9.30 US standard dry cups of freshly squeezed insect excrement for their personal consumption every day. Except the sixth and seventh days, though. They got twice as much on the sixth day, and nothing on the seventh, because God didn't do 7-day trading back then.

So anyway, God commands the people to eat up all their lovely bug shit and not save any for the next day, but some people (of course) did not listen and tried to save some of it, only to find that, *"it was full of maggots and began to smell"* (Ex. 16:20). Not really surprising when you think about it. If you have 600,000 people and animals in a hot desert, you're going to have flies. A LOT of flies. Among other things, these flies will be attracted to the honeydew as a source of nutrition and even incubation for any eggs they lay. The eggs hatch into larvae, find themselves swimming in sugar, and quickly grow into those lovely white squirmies you don't want to find in your Rogan Josh. Honeydew also promotes the growth of a sooty black mould that will certainly smell if left to develop. So, what of the sixth and seventh day dilemma? Why didn't the stuff go off after a day like it usually did? Well, beyond a creative Alteration of the Truth, we could suppose that the refugeebrews found a way to keep the stuff out of the heat and covered to prevent the flies from attacking it, allowing them to extend its use-by date, even if it's just one day.

We are told that, *"some people went out on the seventh day to gather it, but found none"* (Ex. 16:27), but how truthful is that? Sure, "some people" found none on the seventh day, but is that because that particular patch had already been harvested? Or perhaps there weren't any bugs on the bushes in that search area? It's also likely that the movement of 600,000 people and livestock effectively trampled any bug poo that might have been there. Whatever the reason is, we can be certain that this particular part is open to wide interpretation, although I would hazard a guess that the original author/editor of the bible was a big fan of the whole "seventh day resting" thing, even if it meant working like a dog on the sixth day to compensate for it, or he was just outright adulterating the truth.

As a result of those less believing going out on the seventh day to score their bugshit, God is all like, *"How long will you refuse to keep my commands and my instructions?"* (Ex. 16:28). He goes on about how he "gave" them the Sabbath, and why he generously doles out two helpings of bugshit on the sixth day, and that no one is to go out on the seventh. Well, yeah okay, fine; but what difference does it make to God's plans if people are out and about on a Sabbath? It's not like it's God's golf day and he's protecting the Chosen Peeps from his vicious hook shots. How would it in any way, shape or form mess with his Divine Plan if someone wants to get some fresh air of a weekend? And really, if the Sabbath was that strictly enforced, why is it that God's followers go to their respective churches on that Sabbath, or knock on your door to bother you with their holy mission to convert heathens and infidels (i.e. you)? Depending on their particular faith/cult, the Sabbath could be anything from Friday to Sunday, but regardless of the day, the sin of going out is committed by these followers. Perhaps it's just a failing within Humanity that we can't follow the simplest of instructions, stemming back from those times? Who can know for sure?

Random Side Thought: Why do people go to churches to commune with God at all? Isn't he supposed to be omnipresent? Since when do you have to go to a particular building to attract his attention? If God was truly omnipresent, it wouldn't matter where you were, or what you were doing, a simple happy-clap would gain an audience with him. But not only are we told that we have to go to a brick building every Sunday (or whenever) to be "saved," God also demands our money as well. Perhaps because God hasn't got a Tax File Number, or he's just not that savvy with finances. As a child I was taken to church/Sunday School, and it was confusing and frustrating at the same time. You would stand there in a cold, stuffy building full of people where some old git in a dress would pontificate from a podium – 100% uninteresting to the average seven-year-old child – and then the nearest parent to you would drop some money in your hand (usually about 20 cents). And then, just when you had figured out how many of each lolly you were going to buy at the local delicatessen (two Chicos, four racecars and a python, rounding up with Smarties and a freckle), some arsehole with a plate would come along and want you to hand that money over. "Piss off, this is *my* hard-given money!!" would be the standard seven-year-old response.

Luckily, shortly afterward a local soccer club was established and, hearing that matches were played on a Sunday, was eagerly embraced and allowed me to dodge church for the next eight years; by which time I was almost out of high school and able to make my own choices about how to spend my Sunday, none of which involved dress-wearing pontificators or plate-wielding extortionists.

Back to the narrative. Moses then says *"This is what the LORD has commanded: 'Take an omer of manna and keep it for the generations to come, so they can see the bread I gave you to eat in the wilderness when I brought you out of Egypt.'"* (Ex. 16:32). Then he says it to Aaron (Ex. 16:33). A bit of double-redundancy there, but whatever; the point is that God apparently wants a jar of bugshit to be kept so that everyone will know that God made them eat bug shit and that they should be bloody well grateful for it. Soo, does this jar exist today, I can't help but wonder? Is it still intact, and the bug shit still fresh? If it's a sacred relic, as we are led to infer by the ritual keeping of this for "generations to come," then surely it's out there somewhere? What better way to prove these events happened than to go and find the jar that contains the Holy Bug Poo, perfectly preserved and edible? Or is this relic only accessible to the Hebrew people for their validations? Surely, this was intended to show beyond doubt that there is only one true God, otherwise what would be the point of the exercise? According to Wikipedia, the jar was "lost" during the Siege of Jerusalem circa 577 BCE, with some occult tales of a priest finding clues to its whereabouts only to "drop dead" before being able to reveal the location of the jar, reminiscent of Egyptian curses supposedly protecting various pyramids which we are told are the burial tombs of the pharaohs, despite the evidence to the contrary. For a scintillating rundown on the pyramids and their supposed role in ancient society, I highly recommend watching a series called The Pyramid Code, currently streaming on Netflix as I author this book. But for now, let us resume our narrative.

Then comes the following passage: *"As the LORD commanded Moses, Aaron put the manna with the tablets of the covenant law, so that it might be preserved"* (Ex. 16:34).

So Aaron, on Moses' command, put the jar with the Tablets of Covenant Law. He put the manna jar with the stone tablets upon which the Ten Commandments were written. Problem: how can Aaron have placed the manna with the tablets *when they haven't been created yet?!* Aren't we jumping ahead of ourselves just a tiny little bit here? If the Good Book is supposed to be an accurate, transcribed record of what went down all those centuries ago – as billions of Christians would have you believe – then how the hell can the tablets possibly have been referenced prior to their creation? Someone is either jumping ahead to explain where the manna jar was eventually kept, or they're just making it up as they go along, and they've forgotten that they haven't written that part of the story yet! But then, we're not averse to the bible's penchant for not adhering to a cohesive timeline, are we readers? We need only think back to Joseph's magical silver soothsaying cup, which was specifically described and recognized in Gen. 44:6, despite not being actually "discovered" in Benny's sack until 44:12 (insert any number of double-entendres here). I mean really, if we're supposed to believe the bible is an accurate account of our early history, they should have at least tried to preserve the integrity of the timeline, if at least to maintain some semblance of credibility.

In our final passage, we are told that the refugeebrews ate manna for forty years (Ex. 16:35), until they reached the border of Canaan. As if eating bugshit for forty years is something to be particularly proud of, but I suppose it's a perfect example of, "to each, his own."

Moving on.

Exodus 17: Of Rocky Water and More Slaughtered Innocents

"We will not learn how to live together in peace by killing each other's children." -Jimmy Carter

We begin this chapter with Moses leading the refugeebrews out of the Desert of Sin into the lands of Canaan, wandering from place to place according to the whims of their schizophrenic god, eventually reaching the land of Rephidim where, apparently, there was no water to drink (Ex. 17:1). On arrival at this liquidly-bereft place (yes, "arid" is better, but I don't care), Moses' peeps started whining like little bitches again – no surprises there – and demanded of Moses and Aaron, *"Give us water to drink,"* to which Moses replied, *"Why do you quarrel with me? Why do you put the LORD to the test?"* (Ex. 17:2). Well, perhaps it's because your "Lord" has been putting you all through proverbial hoops ever since you started on this asinine odyssey is why, Mose. Or have you already forgotten all the bullshit you had to go through with the Pharaoh and his Adamantium heart and so on, you dense mofo?

Anyway, none of this alters the fact that over half a million people and animals are dying of thirst and that they're all blaming Moses for their predicament. They're all like, *"Why did you bring us up out of Egypt to make our children and livestock die of thirst?"* and waah, waah, waah

(Ex. 17:3). So Moses, with reliable predictability, in turn whines to God, saying, *"What am I to do with these people? They are almost ready to stone me"* (Ex. 17:4). Bloody whining mob of whiners, it's a wonder God didn't just Ski-doosh the lot of 'em like he did at Sodom and Gomorrah.

Despite this overwhelming temptation of his own, God instead says, *"Go out in front of the people. Take with your some of the elders of Israel and take the staff with which you struck the Nile, and go. I will stand there before you by the rock at Horeb. Strike the rock, and water will come out of it for the people to drink"* (Ex. 17:5 – 17:6). Okay, so God is going to physically stand there next to Mose while he performs his aquatic feat of conjuration. Just so we're clear on that, based on what the Book claims. So Moses performs his stick-trick in front of the elders and summons the promised water from the rock, calling the place Massah and Meribah – despite already having named the bloody place Rephidim - because the Israelites quarreled (read: bitched and moaned) and because they tested the LORD saying, *"Is the LORD among us or not?"* (Ex. 17:6 – 17:7).

Well, if God was kickin' it next to Mose when he did his magic trick, that should have been more than sufficient evidence for the elders to be convinced of God's existence, surely? The naming of this place by two names is overkill, but I suppose it depends on whether you want to name it after the "miracle" of the water coming from the rock, or by the fact that the refrugeebrews were whining like little whiners as per usual. And since when is God willing to submit to the tests of mere humans? The merest wave of his smitey finger should be more than enough to prove his existence and alleged omnipotence, so what's the deal with having to "prove" his existence? It's nonsensical in the extreme for this God character to repeatedly prove his existence in the distant past and yet be utterly uninvolved (and unprovable) today. Religionism would be on a lot firmer ground if their God occasionally came down and zapped the odd Hitler or two, or righted a wrong, or cured a kid of bone cancer, or generally acted like he gave a shit about us as he claims. And I'm not talking about having something happen and having it instantly attributed it to divine intervention with no supporting evidence. I'm talking about the Big Guy himself rocking up to the hospital/crisis/war/whatever, proclaiming to several independent witnesses, "Hey homies, wazzup, G-man here, gonna cure me some kiddy cancer today, check this shit out..!" and performing the miracle in question before loping off to his cloud to chill, and perhaps tossing some more bug shit over the side for us to eat. Then I would have more truck with it.

But unless and until such a thing happens, any such happenings are pure serendipity.

The Amalekites Defeated

So it turns out that, apparently, a tribe of peeps called the Amalekites weren't happy with Mose and his homies coming out of the desert and usurping their lands, so they banded together and attacked them at Rephedim, or Massah or Meribah or whatever they felt like calling the place at the time (Ex. 17:8). A perfectly normal thing for them to do, really, in a time of tribal-centric living where xenophobic tendencies were still being given free rein. Anyway, they did this, and so Moses grabbed Joshua and told him, *"Choose some of our men and go out and fight the Amalekites. Tomorrow I will stand on top of the hill with the staff of God in my hands"* (Ex. 17:9). Hmm. My first question would be, if you're being attacked by enemies, why would you wait until the next day to bring out your magic God Stick? Despite the fact that it was Moses and his mob that were the true interlopers, he feels justified in calling these people "enemy" despite having no contact with them prior to this.

Or did they? A quick search of Amalekites reveals something very interesting: apparently, the Amalekites were founded by someone by the name of, predictably, Amalek, who just happens to be a grandson of Esau, the poor sap who got cheated out of both his birthright *and* his blessing by Jacob/Israel/whatever back in Genesis. So we're not talking about a random skirmish here, but a generational blood feud, where Jacob/Israel/whatever's descendants are still pounding on Esau's blood lines, trying to wipe them off the planet at every opportunity despite robbing them of their birthrights and blessings and pretty much anything else that isn't nailed down. Talk about holding a grudge, just because Esau was Isaac's favoured son! I've said it before, and I'll say it again: Jacob's line has *issues*. Really big ones.

Anyway, back to the story. Joshua toddles off and fights the Amalekites while Moses, Aaron and some random fucker named Hur went up to the hill (apparently, he was Moses' nephew from Miriam and 3-IC after Aaron). While he's up there, Moses notices that while his arms are raised, the Israelites would be winning; but if he dropped his arms, the Amalekites would gain the upper hand (pun intended). Eventually Moses got tired, so Aaron and Hur plonked a rock down for him to sit on, and between the two of them they held Moses' arms up for him, thereby allowing Joshua to overcome the Amalekite army with the sword (Ex. 17:11 – 17:13). Yeah, great. Then, *"the LORD said to Moses, 'Write this on a scroll as something to be remembered and make sure that Joshua hears it, because I will completely blot out the name of Amalek from under heaven'"* (Ex. 17:14). Then Moses built another bloody altar, calling it The LORD is my Banner (pff!), and then claimed that, *"because hands were lifted up against the throne of the LORD, the LORD will be at war with the Amalekites from generation to generation"* (Ex. 17:16).

For what, pray? What did Esau do against this God that was so wrong that he would have his descendants marked for extermination forever after? Hmm, well I suppose he did marry two Canaanite women, which may have ruffled a few feathers back in Noah's day when he cursed Canaan in a post-bender hissy-fit. It just goes to show how long these psychotic, inbred arsehats have held onto this grudge. Let it go, Elsa!

From an objective viewpoint, it would appear that the idea of God has been used, in general and in this chapter in particular, to justify the genocide of innocents since the Dawn of Man. I know you're sitting back right now thinking to yourself, "Well, duh, I could have told you that for free," and you'd be right. But it's refreshing to point out this reality using the very book religious fanatics use to proclaim God's eternal love for mankind, provided you toe his line … and give him your money, of course.

Exodus 18: Daddy-in-Law Puts In His Two Shekels, Gets Referenced Repeatedly

"And I don't like books which are full of name dropping." -Daphne du Maurier

In some ways this is an unrelated side-chapter, probably just an effort to flesh out a very dodgy storyline and distract the reader's concentration for long enough to make them forget the many inconsistencies scattered throughout the bible. In this one, we're treated to the story of "Jethro, Moses' father-in-law," a phrase that is repeated on no less than five separate occasions, in case you missed it the first time. Perhaps the original author of these ancient texts had some dealings with this Jethro, and was slipped a few shekels to, "make sure they know I was his father-in-law, okay? The chicks'll really dig that!" or words to that effect. I cordially dare anyone to prove otherwise. Interesting, too, how Moses' father-in-law was first referenced in Ex.4 when he wanted to sod off to Egypt, but not by any name. Why not, if it's so vitally important it be mentioned in this chapter? Odd.

Anyway, Jethro (Moses' father-in-law, just in case you missed that bit) had by this time heard everything that had gone on since Mose left for Egypt to free his peeps from the Pharaoh. Then we're treated with 18:2: *"After Moses had sent away his wife Zipporah, his father-in-law Jethro* (in case you missed it the first two times) *received her and her two sons."* Okay, when the hell did that happen, exactly? Last we heard anything of Zippo, she was hacking at her son's junk with a flint knife and rubbing it vigorously on her husband to gross out a murderous god intent on killing him. What happened then? Occam's Flint Knife would suggest that Mose sent her away then, her deed done and, from the tone of her words, disgusted with the fact she had to mutilate her child. This would not have pleased Mose and the G-man and, while it's not covered anywhere in the scriptures, it's probable that Mose had a pow-wow with G-man (or, more than likely, himself) and packed her off to her father for being an uppity bitch. Whatever, this thing happened, and most likely at the time of the impromptu flint flensing.

Then we're treated to some interpretations. Ex.18:3 and 18:4 describes: *"One son was named Gershom, for Moses said, 'I have become a foreigner in a foreign land'; and the other was named Eliezer, for he said, 'My father's God was my helper; he saved me from the sword of Pharaoh.'"*

Hmm.

Now, anyone who has ever picked up a Big Book of Baby Names realizes that names have some original meaning in whatever language they happen to have originated from. For instance, "Bonnie" typically originates from the Scottish word for, "beautiful," and something like "Stephen" translates as, "crown" or "king," and so on and so forth (I'm sure you've been there and done that, readers, so I won't go on). But I'm having a hard time reconciling Eliezer with the given meaning. Next thing we know, they'll be trying to convince us that "Moses" actually means, "persecuted Hebrew baby left in the reeds by the Nile to be found by Pharaoh's daughter who raised it as her own using his natural mother as a wet-nurse but they didn't know it because it was all an elaborate ruse perpetrated by his sister Miriam who then went on to kill an Egyptian and wander the wilderness for 40 years before freeing his people from the aforementioned Pharaoh and wandering the desert for another 40 years."

I dare anyone to prove otherwise.

Enough of this, moving on with this annoying chapter. Jethro, father-in-law to Moses (in case you missed it the first three times), along with Zippo and sons, came to Moses in the wilderness where he was camped out under the Mountain of God; apparently this was the case, because Jethro had sent word to him, *"I, your father-in-law Jethro* (in case you missed it the first four times), *am coming to you with your wife and her two sons"* (Ex. 18:6).

135

Her two sons? Not "your" two sons, but "her"..? Has Moses disowned his kids? Did he lose custody in the divorce? Well, no, she's still referred to has his wife, so that's not it. With the bible so heavily weighted towards having sons and regarding women to be mere chattel and generally being male ego-centric, it seems odd for this to be here, giving Zippo ownership of Moses' offspring. Let's not forget when Jacob (Israel, whatever) chastised his son for going, *"up onto your father's bed, onto my couch, and defiling it"* back in Gen. 49:4, referring of course to Reuben's rodgering of Jacob's concubine Bilbah/Bilhah/whatever. Given these attitudes, I expect the writing of, "her" is erroneous, but it was something that caught the eye, as they say.

Moving on. Moses apparently went out to meet his father-in-law and bowed down and kissed him (makes you wonder what part of his father-in-law he kissed!), greetings were exchanged and then they went into the tent (Ex. 18:7). No mention of reuniting with his wife and sons, though. Odd. Anyway, Mose regales his dad-in-law with All the Happenings since he hoofed it back to Egypt to free his homies, and what G-man had done (or hadn't done) to help Moses on his quest. Jethro was either fed some adulterated tale or he wasn't that good of a listener, because he was delighted at all the good things G-man had done, praising him for rescuing Moses and the peeps from Pharaoh and the Egyptians, adding, *"Now I know that the LORD is greater than all other gods, for he did this to those who had treated Israel arrogantly"* (Ex. 18:11).

Another mention of "other gods." The bible is supposed to be the Record of Creation by one god. One, not many. Now we could argue that these others are man-made, "false gods," but if we play Devil's Advocate, there must've been some witnessing, some display of power, that convinced the peoples of the time that there were other gods floating about. Yes, the people then were rather primitive and partial to wild, unverified speculation about things like storms, floods, droughts, or any number of happenings in their environment; but what makes this God of the Hebrews so different to those other gods? The assertion that he walked among us during those early days and interacted with Adam and Noah and Crazy Old Abe and so on? If that is the case, why doesn't he do that now? Are we so different in our makeup today that we could not withstand a direct face-to-face? If the only condition of a personal audience is to be good and blameless, there are plenty of people on the planet today that would qualify, schizophrenic tendencies notwithstanding. Which wouldn't be the case if you could turn around and point and say, "Look, here he is; Hi, G..!" And we are still waiting for the introduction of Satan, or the Devil, or Beelzebub, or whatever your term is for God's nemesis/fallen angel/whatever. I can't help but wonder why he hasn't turned up yet, but rest assured we'll cover that notable if and when he rocks up to create his havoc.

For now, though, we return to this boring chapter. Then Jethro, Moses' father-in-law (in case you missed it the first eight times), *"brought burnt offerings and other sacrifices to God, and Aaron came with all the elders of Israel to eat a meal with Moses' father-in-law* (that's Jethro, if you missed it the first twenty times) *in the presence of God"* (Ex. 18:12). Are we to infer from this passage that God was physically present at this meal? Or merely an invisible observer? If the meal was to celebrate God's "good work" in the Freeing of the Peeps, it seems a bit harsh not to let G-man enjoy some of the repast on offer. It's like being at your birthday party but you're not allowed to have any of your cake.

Let's look further for some more clues. The next day, Moses installs himself as Judge for the People, and they (the people, I guess) stood around him from morning to evening. When Jethro (his father-in-law in case you missed it the first fifty times) saw what Mose was doing and asked him why, Mose replied that it was because the people have come to him to seek God's will. *"Whenever they have a dispute, it is brought to me, and I decide between the parties and inform them of God's decrees and instructions"* (Ex.

18:16). Hmm, judge, jury and executioner, if I have the right of it here, backed up by a God that, despite washing his hands of Humanity just after the flood, has been meddling in it constantly ever since. G-man, you either have to back the fuck up and leave us to sort our own mess out, or you get off your fucking cloud and dominate us with your totalitarian smitey finger. You can't have it both ways, dude. And if we adhere to the idea that God does not exist, then we're left with someone who talks to bushes and invisible beings that aren't really there, getting themselves installed as a leader of the people and making morality judgments for them because they don't have the ear of God to guide them. Kinda sounds like every country in the world today that hasn't maintained the separation between Church and State, doesn't it?

Anyway, Jethro (who was, if you recall, Moses' father-in-law, you might've missed that the first three hundred times) says to Moses that, *"What you are doing is not good,"* explaining that the people will remain unsatisfied and that Moses will burn himself out under the strain; before recommending that Moses pick a few capable men – *"men who fear God, trustworthy men who hate dishonest gain"* – to deal with all the simpler disputes, leaving Moses with the difficult ones to hash out with the G-man personally. So, essentially, delegating authority. Moses goes along with this idea (Ex. 18:17 – 18:24) before packing Jethro off back to his own country (Ex. 18:27).

And another chapter bites the dust. It was most certainly boring, and needlessly repetitive, but I cover it purely because it's there and it would be a piss-poor interpretation if I cherry-picked the verses and chapters I had particular issues with while ignoring the rest. And who knows, it could still have some interesting relevance later on, and then you'd be annoyed at me for skipping it, yes? And if all else fails, it's given me an extra eight pages for my book. Huzzah!

Exodus 19: At Mount Sinai, and Some Extremely Interesting Precautions

"The Jews would have us believe that God had this bias to this little small tribe in the middle of the Sinai desert, and all the rest of humanity is just rubbish. I mean, that is the basic doctrine of the Jewish religion, and that's why it is a most racist religion." -Hamza Yusuf

In the wake of the last chapter, you could be forgiven for thinking that we've degraded into a boring, routine breakdown of Exodus. And if you've read my first offering, you're probably wondering what happened to my alternative "Spaceman Scenario" to which I referred on a more-than-casual basis, lending some romance and high-tech possibilities to the subject matter. Well, put on your tinfoil hats and strap your Velcro tightly, because this chapter promises to be all that and more! Let's dive in, shall we?

We start with the refugeebrews finally arriving at the Desert of Sinai, *"three months to the day after they left Egypt,"* and summarily pitching their tents at the base of Mount Sinai (19:1 – 19:2). Wait, what...?! This makes a mockery of their previously stated claims of their forty-year wandering being completed in Ex. 17:1, where they left the Desert of Sin and entered the lands of Canaan! Additionally, Ex. 16:35 *specifically* said that they ate bugshit for forty years, until they reached the border of Canaan; meaning that, for all intents and purposes, they had left their desert wanderings behind them. It's okay, I'll wait here while you go and verify that for yourselves … dum-de-dummm…. there, you see?! Someone's spinning shit, and for once it isn't Yours Truly..!

Okay, onward. So Moses, *"went up to God, and the LORD called to him from the mountain,"* and told him, *"what you are to say to the descendants of Jacob and what you are tell the people of Israel"* (Ex. 19:3). Hmm. From the way that's worded, it's almost like God has two separate instructions for the groups in question. Ahhh, but when has God ever told one person a thing, and then told someone else another thing? Or gone and done something else? Never mind that for now. Then we read, *"You yourselves have seen what I did to Egypt, and how I carried you on eagles' wings and brought you to myself"* (Ex. 19:4).

How very interesting. Where did the eagle come from? Why hasn't there been any mention of ornithological participation before this? Did this eagle carry the entire nation of Israel, or did it just ferry Moses up to God and back? Was it, in fact, an eagle, or did it merely have the shape and sound of one? Was this "eagle" a one-man jet-propelled craft piloted remotely from God's orbiting spacecraft or similar? We know that jet engines do not function outside of the planet's atmosphere (no oxygen) but we could suppose that it possessed dual-engine capability, or even retrofitted to utilize liquidized oxygen from a storage tank to achieve combustion in space. We're not there just yet as a species, but we're getting there fast with the work being done by Elon Musk and his ilk. And should this be the case, a jet engine winding up could achieve the kind of pitch reminiscent of a screaming eagle to the average uneducated goat herder. It's food for thought.

So God then promises that, if the Israelites obey him fully and keep his covenants, they will be his *"treasured possession"* out of all the nations on earth (Ex. 19:5). Then expands it a bit by saying, *"Although the whole earth is mine, you will be for me a kingdom of priests and a holy nation"* (Ex. 19:6). Basically saying to Moses, "It's all mine, but screw those other guys, I love my Hebies." But therein lies the problem. We're not that far into the history of the bible: we've dug our way through Genesis, and only a short way through Exodus, but the (bible) fact is that all nations originated from Noah and his family, and further back to Adam. So therefore, every human on earth should be related in some way or another, according to religion; therefore, we should all be accorded equal favour in God's eyes. Black, white, yellow, brown, purple, pink, brindled, it's just the wrapping and should not matter one iota. Whether you have a foreskin or not isn't a matter of genetics, and getting it hacked off doesn't turn you into another race of beings that get greater benefits than others. God should just quit playing favourites and stop being an arsehat, unless of course my Garden of Eden interpretation has any basis in fact (see my previous book for details) and God did in fact create a new genetic species from a group of ape-like hominids already on the cusp of humanity; or that this particular group was clear of the inbreeding perpetrated by the crew of God's ship and so were more genetically "pure" than the rest of the world's humans. We weren't there, we don't know, and we can only speculate based on the available data; but it may explain some of God's tendency to play favourites.

So, Moses went back to the elders of Israel and passed on everything he was told. *"The people then all responded together, 'We will do everything the LORD has said'"* (Ex.19:8). So Moses brought their answer back to the LORD - six hundred thousand people plus women and children, all responding at once; I would imagine God would have heard that racket, and what a feat of timing that would have been in any case – and then the fun begins.

God then says to Moses, *"I am going to come to you in a dense cloud, so that the people will hear me speaking with you and will always put their trust in you"* (Gen. 19:9). Why a "dense cloud?" God hasn't needed one of those before, and he hasn't necessarily been shy in showing himself to people before, unless being seen by six hundred thousand people was giving him serious stage fright. Whatevs, G-man, do what you gotta do, what else are you going to tell us, I wonder? As it turns out, some interesting preparations that have been relabeled as, "Consecrations."

God tells Moses to go and *"consecrate the people today and tomorrow."* Then the following, in no particular order (Ex.19:10 – 19:15):

- Have them wash their clothes and be ready by the third day, because on that day the LORD will come down on Mount Sinai in the sight of all the people;

- Put limits for the people around the mountain, and do not approach the mountain or touch the foot of it;

- Whoever touches the mountain is to be put to death;

- They are to be stoned or shot with arrows; not a hand is to be laid on them;

- No person or animal shall be permitted to live;

- Only when the ram's horn sounds a long blast may they approach the mountain;

- Abstain from sexual relations.

Now I don't know about you guys, but to me this sounds like a Radiation Contamination Protocol. Wash the clothes, so that if there is contamination it will show. Keeping the people away from the source of the radiation. Killing the people who get irradiated, in such a manner that further radiation exposure is minimized, including corpse management. Abstaining from sex to prevent women from suffering birth abnormalities in the event of exposure in the first day or two of conception. And a long horn blast when the risk of radiation exposure has passed. We've seen this stuff every day in our popular culture since we figured out how to split the atom, and it cannot be a coincidence that these measures are handed down to Moses prior to "God's" descent to earth. If you have a more rational explanation for these instructions, I'm open to suggestions, but for now let's run with this and see where it takes us.

Moses relays all this information and does all the consecration things and, on the third day, *"there was thunder and lightning, with a thick cloud over the mountain, and a very loud trumpet blast"* (Ex. 19:16). Stands to reason. Thunder of course being the sound generated from whatever means of propulsion God had at his disposal, the thick cloud indicative of thrust from those engines, and the odd bit of lightning indicating static discharge, perhaps, or they could have put that in there as a fancy, because where there is thunder, there is typically lightning. So Moses gathered his peeps and trudged them to the foot of the mountain and waited to meet with God. *"Mount Sinai was covered with smoke, because the LORD descended on it in fire. The smoke billowed up from it like smoke from a furnace, and the whole mountain trembled violently"* (Ex. 19:18).

Again, it's self-explanatory. Smoke everywhere, and not "dense cloud" as hitherto claimed in Ex. 19:9, but clouds can be dust or water or smoke so it still counts, I suppose. Lots and lots of dense, hot smoke due to the thrust needed to control the speed of his descent to something approaching survivability. And the whole mountain trembling violently because of the transfer of kinetic energy from the engines to the ground. Anyone lucky enough to have seen a rocket launch from Cape Canaveral will know what it feels like, I'm sure, only imagine that in reverse. So anyway, God touches down, the trumpet became louder (not a ram's horn any more, but a trumpet), and when Moses called out to God, he answered, calling Moses to the top of the mountain, at which point Mose hoofed it up the hill (Ex. 19:19 – 19:20). All good so far, no dramas.

When Moses arrives at the top, God tells him to, *"Go down and warn the people so they do not force their way through to see the LORD and many of them perish"* (Ex. 19:21). Yeah, good one G; make the old bastard hoof it all the way up the mountainside only to go back down again and keep his horde of nosy onlookers at bay. Seriously dude, if you were able to call Moses up the mountain, surely you could have told the rest of 'em *not* to come up and save him the extra trips on his old plates'o'meat. Appalling behaviour, treating the elderly like that. Then, *"Even the priests, who approach the LORD, must consecrate themselves, or he will break out against them"* (Ex. 19:22).

Interesting choice of the phrase, "break out." If what I've read about radiation poisoning is accurate, you can expect a range of nasty symptoms including, but not limited to, weakness, fatigue and confusion; and more excitingly, bleeding from the orifices, bruising, burns, open sores and even sloughing of the skin (leprosy, anyone?), hair loss, swelling and other such wonders, depending on severity of exposure. It's a pretty good way of appearing omnipotent – keep away or I'll fuck you up! – and then claim that the resulting bodily destruction is the Will of God or something. Anyway, Moses reminds God that he's already told the people not to approach the mountain on pain of death and nastiness. So God then commands Moses to, *"go down and bring Aaron up with you. But the priests and the people must not (blah blah, break out blah blah)"*, and Moses went down and told them (Ex. 19:24 – 19:25), and that's the end of that chapter.

So how do you feel about the validity of the Spaceman Scenario, readers? Does it hold more water, the longer we consider the technological discoveries humanity has made since the bible was written? I can't help but feel there's some element of truth to it, obviously, or I wouldn't be sitting here typing it all out for you to enjoy. But whatever really happened all those years ago, it's interesting to note that Mount Sinai (or parts thereof) is to this very day fenced off from outsiders and patrolled by armed guards. Signs at the fence claim it to be an "Archeological Site" and indeed it is, so it's perhaps normal to want to prevent klutzy tourists from disturbing items of significance or making off with bits of rock they think is a bit of smashed tablet. Others suggest that it's been fenced off to deter advocates of other religions destroying things that may prove their own religion to be false. And still others think it's a government cover up akin to Area 51, hiding evidence that an advanced species set foot on our planet and left its mark.

What you believe, dear readers, is entirely up to you.

Exodus 20: The Ten Commandments (at least, to start with)

"I have wondered at times what the Ten Commandments would have looked like if Moses had run them through the US Congress." -Ronald Reagan

So now we've finally reached that one part of the bible that everyone on the planet should at least be partially familiar with: the giving of the ten commandments to Moses atop Mount Sinai. And while it would be fun to imagine Chucky Heston paused over a tablet with a hammer and chisel transcribing these commandments – "Is 'commandment' one M or two, oh Lord..?" – this isn't that part, at least not yet. No, this is God merely telling Moses these laws, for him to go down and recite to all the Chosen Peeps a'la Chinese Whispers style. Because people in their eighties can be trusted to remember everything that was said to them, yes? Let's see what we can glean from this.

We begin straight off by God claiming his part in bringing the Hebrews out of slavery. Then, *"You shall have no other gods before me"* (Ex. 20:3). So, God himself concedes that there are other gods about the place. How would that even have happened when God – this god – created the entire universe and everything in it? And why would he go to the effort of creating other gods to potentially rival his omnipotence if he's so bloody jealous and possessive? This doesn't make sense unless these gods were created by Man. And if they were created, then how much of this saga is also a man-made fantasy?

Okay, next one: *"You shall not make for yourself an image in the form of anything in heaven above or on the earth beneath or in the waters below"* (Ex.20:4). Well, damn, that means everyone that has ever attended a church is in deep shit. How many times have we seen huge effigies of Jesus on his cross behind the podium? Worshippers the world over bow down to this effigy, and yet Commandment Two specifically forbids this! There are no exceptions or caveats here – no, "oh, but you can do it with images of me" – the banning of images is in its entirety, and as such every God-fearing Christian is breaking this commandment with every God/Jesus/Mary (circle applicable) idol they tack onto the wall or put in a niche. They are all of them engaging in forbidden Idolatry and are going to burn in hell, apparently. Assuming we ever get to the parts of the bible that describe this place, because up until now it's been God that's doing the punishing; he hasn't delegated that task to a third party as yet.

Commandment Two, Addendum: *"You shall not bow down to them or worship them; for I, the LORD your God, am a jealous God, punishing the children for the sin of the parents to the third and fourth generations of those who hate me, but showing love to a thousand generations of those who love me and keep my commandments"* (Ex. 20:5 – 20:6). Again, jealous god, creates other gods and then hates on the people who worship these other gods that God himself created. Makes perfect sense. Also, any Christian who worships his idolatry not only condemns him or herself, but their descendants for up to four generations. Way to go, wingnut!

There's also the issue of those who "love" God and obey him, passing that on for a thousand generations. Is that guaranteed? What if I'm the 500th generation, say, and I succumb to base Idol worship? Does that mean I suffer the same fate as those who "hate" God? I'm only half way through the 1000-generation love-fest from the devotion of my ancestors, so how could I be punished for my idolatry when I'm still under the Extended Warranty, so to speak? Of course, you'd have to have kept accurate records or at least a receipt of how your great-great-great-great-etc.-grandparents loved God's guts and did no wrong before you make a claim on this loophole. It could end badly.

Commandment Three: *"You shall not misuse the name of the LORD your God, for the LORD will not hold anyone guiltless who misuses his name"* (Ex. 20:7). So something as innocuous as, "Oh, for God's sake!" is technically a misuse. Or is it?

Whatever happens is according to God's Divine Plan™ (remember that little ditty?), therefore it would be absolutely correct to place the blame for any adversities you're experiencing on that doorstep. To be fair, it's usually his son that cops the majority of disparaging utterances, so I don't know what God's problem is with this, especially when we can use the handy loophole I mentioned earlier (remember, keep receipts).

Commandment Four: *"Remember the Sabbath day by keeping it holy"* (Ex. 20:8). This one was a bit short, so God elaborates further: *"Six days you shall labour ... but the seventh is a Sabbath to the LORD your God. On it you shall not do any work, neither you, nor your son or daughter, nor your male or female servant, nor your animals, nor any foreigner residing in your towns"* (Ex. 20:10), going on to explain that he made everything in six days and bludged on the seventh, so every other bastard can do it as well.

Question: All very well to stop your immediate family from working on the sabbath, but how are you going to convince your *animals* to toe the line (or hoof the line/claw the line/etc.)? Animals have no concept of religion, nor are they capable of such thought. What if you left your camels in their plough traces overnight and when you get up on the sabbath, they've gone and ploughed your entire field all by themselves? And in the act of defecation, they've also turned that into the soil and thus effectively fertilized it too? Ooooh man, God's gonna give you a royal arse-kicking for that, and all because you were too tired to put your camels away for the weekend. Sucks to be you.

The same applies to any "foreigners" in your town. They don't follow your cult, so how are you going to make them toe the line without resorting to oppressive and violent means? It's no wonder the more fundamentally religious places of the world are so dangerous for the average traveler. Your most innocent action, something you might have done unconsciously all your life, could be perceived as heresy and you wouldn't even know it until you're forcibly manhandled onto a chopping block with a machete whistling down towards your neck. Thanks, but no thanks. While I totally agree with judging a person based on behaviour, it should be based on rational, normal things like because they've stolen or raped or murdered someone, not because they let their wife walk in front of them or they baked a cake on a Sunday. It's not that hard to be rational, guys. Seriously.

Commandment Five: *"Honour your father and your mother, so that you may live long in the land the LORD your God is giving you"* (Ex. 20:12). Well that's fair enough, you should always respect your parents, because they brought you into the world, after all, and raised you with varying degrees of success. Some may argue that their parents were complete arsehats, or drug-fucked losers or abusive or whatnot, and that's always a Bad Thing. But you don't have to like them; you don't even have to love them. You only have to respect the fact that they are your birth parents, otherwise you wouldn't be alive. No matter where you run or hide, there is no escaping that ancestry; so while you might hate their guts, you need to reconcile their part in your creation within yourself or it will just poison your heart and you will end up passing that disrespect onto your own children, who will end up not respecting anything or anyone.

Commandment Six: *"You shall not murder"* (Ex. 20:13). Another solid one, here. I can't help but think of some worthy caveats to this, such as removing a paedophile or a thief from society, but the basic premise is good.

Commandment Seven: *"You shall not commit adultery"* (Ex. 20:14). A fair call, love the one you're with, after all. There's no point marrying a chick if you're just going to have it off with her slave girl, after all (yeah, I'm looking at you, Abe). So does this signify the end of concubines in Abrahamic religion? Umm, no. There are references of its continued practice after these events, in particular by David, self-appointed king of Hebron, who, *"took more concubines and wives in Jerusalem"* (2 Samuel 5:13), after his infamous rock-flinging incident with Goliath. I suppose he thought that, after pocking a nine-and-a-half foot giant in the forehead, he had *carte blanche* to shoot his load wherever he pleased. But this polygamy was definitely after the advent of the 10 commandments, so where does that leave David, holy warrior of Israel, in the eyes of this jealous God? Any instances of adultery demanded death, by stoning, of both participants, which would be hilariously ironic considering how David came into his fame in the first place.

Commandment Eight: *"You shall not steal"* (Ex. 20:15). Another solid law. I personally consider thieves to share a rung on the Social Ladder with paedophiles and politicians (which, it has to be said, are just different types of thief). They are the filth of today's society, just as they were then, and society is much better off without them.

Commandment Nine: *"You shall not give false testimony against your neighbour"* (Ex. 20:16). Another fine law, God's really starting to get the hang of it now after a dodgy start. Nobody likes a tattler, especially one who spreads lies for their own amusement, and at your expense. Not as bad as paedophiles or thieves, but they can certainly feel their breath on their heels.

Commandment Ten: *"You shall not covet your neighbour's house. Nor his wife, nor his male or female servants, his ox or his donkey, or anything that belongs to your neighbour"* (Ex. 20:17). Yeah, okay, so don't envy someone else's stuff. Not that there's anything wrong with admiring that stuff, and perhaps making you reevaluate your life choices so that you can have nice stuff of your own one day. I suppose he threw that in there because he didn't trust the Israelites to stop at mere admiration, thinking it would lead to breaking Commandment Eight, followed by Commandment Seven if he was *really* into his ox or donkey, leading to breaking Number Six when the original owner objected violently to his stuff being Seven'ed and Eight'ed. Nice bit of foresight happening there, G, but it doesn't say much about the moral integrity of your Chosen Peeps, does it?

So that's the Ten Commandments done and dusted. God needn't have worried about being mobbed by the Israelites; they were too busy shitting themselves at all the loud thunder and lightning and horns going off to go anywhere near the mountain. Indeed, they said to Moses, *"Speak to us yourself and we will listen. But do not have God speak to us or we will die"* (Ex. 20:19). Why is it that every time something scary or intolerable comes along, they're afraid that they will *die*, every single time? Are these Israelites related in some way to myotonic goats, the ones that go all rigid and fall over when they get a fright? Insanely funny to watch, but ultimately just a genetic mutation. Interesting side-fact: Studies have found that if you deprive these goats of water for three days, the myotonic symptoms completely disappear, and return within 2-3 days when you hydrate them again. Amazing stuff.

Anyway, the Hebes are shit-scared, and Moses tells them to chill out, that God has come to *"test them, so that the Fear of God will be with them to keep them from sinning"* (Ex.20:20). So they all kept the hell away, while Moses went back to the *"thick darkness where God was"* (Ex. 20:21).

So what made Moses so special that he was able to withstand God's scary Death Voice, where others were not? Chosen Champion or not, he's still human and thus susceptible to everything a non-Chosen would be. And we also have the interesting thing of God being in the "thick darkness." Ostensibly it's this dense cloud we were told of earlier, but why dark? Every time we see a religious picture of God, the general consensus is good and clear and above all else, *bright*. Reading God as lurking in the darkness is erroneous, and something more in keeping with what "Satan" would do (Beelzebub, the Devil, Old Scratch, whatever). It would make a rational person question who's really lurking in that cloud, methinks. I've often asked devout Christians over the years if they're worshipping the right guy or not, and that they could in fact be worshipping the devil in disguise. The answer I get most often is, "I just know," bereft of even the smallest rationalization. I usually follow it up with the fact that the devil is the biblical Lord of Deceit, and that he's had such a long time to perfect his illusions that it would be nigh on impossible for a mere human to see through the ruse, as it were. And if we follow the logic, it would be the best way to corrupt humanity; to pose as God, then pass down laws and commandments, some just vague enough to allow differences in interpretation, giving rise to splinter cults who might differ on one minor technicality, but become blood enemies forevermore because of it. Remember, we have over 4,200 distinct religions in the world today, all stemming from some ancient event that's been shrouded in conjecture and hearsay; and who's to say which of these is the truest among them, besides that religion's devotees? Which is all the more reason to abandon the lunacy of Religionism and evolve to embrace Humanism, at least to start, recognizing that we're all in this together and that we should just be the best person we can in the time we have.

Idols, Altars, Genitalia, Everything!

Now that God has read the Riot Act in regards to how the Israelites should behave, he throws in some extra dialogue like any director would with their Extended Footage, Deleted Scenes or whatever you want to call it. He starts off by saying, *"Do not make any gods to be alongside me; do not make for yourselves gods of silver or gods of gold"* (Ex. 20:23). Just a reiteration of the Second Commandment, but if you're a jealous god, you want to make sure of the bits you consider most important. And the part about "making gods" to be alongside him, which puts me in mind of the astute suppositions of Douglas Adams (mayherestinpeace) in that our beliefs create the gods. For a more complete understanding, grab yourself a copy of, "The Long Dark Teatime of the Soul" and enjoy at your leisure, if you have not done so already. I heartily recommend it for both the dark humour and the cutting insight of the human condition we call Life. A brilliant author, gone well before his time.

Next up, God asks to have altars of earth made for him, to accommodate the odd burnt offering of sheep, goats, cattle, firstborn sons, whatever (Ex. 20:24) adding that honouring his Godness will cause him to pop along and bless whoever it is offering up the abovementioned. Yes, okay, I threw in firstborn sons, but we can't leave out the offerings of Crazy Old Abe, can we? Then he mentioned stone altars, which are acceptable per se, so long as the stones aren't dressed. God likes naked stones, okay, whatever turns him on, I guess; adding that the altar builder would, *"defile it if you use a tool on it"* (Ex. 20:25).

Perhaps all this talk of undressed stones and using tools on them was taken euphemistically by God, leading to the next commandment: *"And do not go up to my altar on steps, or your private parts may be exposed"* (Ex. 20:26). In short, God wants your worship, but he doesn't want to see your junk, circumcised or not.

For a god so obsessively phallocentric, it's a strange thing to insist upon. Because lets face it, guys: he created Man in his own image, replete with foreskin, only to have Crazy Old Abe hack it off because God found it distasteful; and now that he's gotten his Chosen Peeps to carve their cocks, dock their dicks, slice their skin-flutes, hack their humpers, wound their wangs, nip their nobs, pare their privates, trim their tockleys, bob their babymakers, flense their funsticks, alter their appendages – insert your favourite euphemism here – God now finds having them in his face offensive. There's just no pleasing this weirdo! Hopefully he'll make up his mind in time for our next chapter, but based on past experience I wouldn't hold my breath.

Exodus 21: Addendums, Provisos, A Few Quid-Pro-Quos

"There are a few, uh, provisos, a, a couple of quid pro quos." -Genie, piss-taking William F. Buckley

Ten Commandments be damned..! It seems that God has had some time to reflect upon his hard-and-fast Ten Commandment regime and figured he needs a caveat or five to better guide Humanity on the more difficult cases regarding bloody, brutal murder, theft, fraud, deception and all the other activities God's Chosen People have been guilty of since Isaac. Today, we all know that we shouldn't kill people – Thou Shalt Not Murder – and yet, would that still be relevant if you're faced with the person who molested and killed your child? Where do we distinguish between the taking of a life, and the fitting recompense for one taken with varying degrees of violence? The line blurs, we begin questioning our moral stance depending on the variables of the situation we find ourselves in. We see someone pounding on an animal, and our sensibilities are immediately outraged and we side with the animal; but if we miss the part where the animal has savagely attacked that person without provocation and bitten their hand down to the bone, we're only getting half the picture. As we are presented with different scenarios in our daily lives, we need to stop and consider that we're only getting half of the picture. An old adage I had growing up was, "Believe nothing of what you hear, and only half of what you see"; if more people adhered to this instead of jumping in half-informed and fully-cocked, social media would not be half as amusing as it is today.

Okay, so to the heart of this chapter, with its myriad addenda, caveats and provisos aimed at softening the rigidity of the Big Ten. God bails up Moses and begins to lay down the Laws that he is to relay to the Israelites. But even here, there are some very interesting interpretations and decisions which no advanced, enlightened being would demand of another person. Let us explore some of these as we find them, shall we?

Hebrew Servants

Gotta love us a good Hebrew slave, yeah? This handy guide will keep you on the straight and narrow, despite them having been "freed" by G in a fit of benevolence. Let's run through the details:

"If you buy a Hebrew servant, he is to serve you for six years. But in the seventh year, he shall go free, without paying anything" (Ex. 21:2). Well, obviously we're talking indentured servitude here, because you'd hardly use the word "buy" when "employ" would better describe a mutual labour-hire situation. And why on earth would that "servant" need to pay for his freedom?

And how would he pay for that freedom when slavery precludes the acquisition of wealth? It's as confusing as it is self-defeating, especially when you consider that the Hebrews are now supposed to be a liberated people.

"If he comes alone, he is to go alone; but if he has a wife when he comes, she is to go with him" (Ex. 21:3). That's fair enough, only leave with what you came with; no need to be relieving your ex-master of his stuff, that's just rude.

Here's an odd one: *"If the master gives him a wife and she bears him sons or daughters, the woman and her children belong to her master, and only the man shall go free"* (Ex. 21:4). Indian-giving at its most heartless. If you've "given" a thing to another person, you've effectively relinquished any rights or ownership you had with the thing in question, be it a trinket or a concubine. So how can you justify retaining ownership of the thing once you no longer control the person you gave the thing to? The idea of women being rented out like the latest movie from Blockbuster is repulsive to us today, despite there being any number of gold-chain-laden entrepreneurs in the lower socio-economic areas of the world becoming very wealthy from the practice.

There is a proviso to this very heartless lending of women to slaves, however. If the freed slave – sorry, *servant* – proclaims love for his master and wife and children, and does not want to go free, then that slave/servant must be brought before "the judges," whoever they are. Then the master must, *take him to the door or the doorpost and pierce his ear with an awl. Then he will be his servant for life"* (Ex. 21:6). Le Ouch. And we're not talking about some nice sharp affair you might encounter next time you want to punch a hole in your tongue for that tongue stud with the smiley face on the ball; if anything, it would've been a rough shard of bronze with an equally rough wooden handle, better suited to poking holes in cow leather than traumatizing your earlobe. Although in retrospect, I suppose it would do a very good job of that indeed, the ungodly screams of pain notwithstanding. Let's agree that it's not very nice, and highlights the continued treatment of people as mere chattel, despite the, "Good Book's" insistence that it is coming from a position of love and tolerance.

As if to reinforce that sentiment: *"If a man sells his daughter as a servant, she is not to go free as male servants do"* (Ex. 21: 7). Well, we're already well aware of the bible's opinion of a woman's worth, what with them being referred to as "couches" and whatnot back in Genesis, when Jacob/Israel/whatever was doing his final bout of soothsaying before kicking the bucket. When you sit back and think about it, I suppose it makes a logical kind of sense that they would hold this opinion of women. The authors of this holy book are moral Neanderthals, and are still pissed off about Applegate and therefore blame all their suffering and stuff on women, whom they consider inferior, treacherous and rib-like; and so they imposed all these less-than-human terms and conditions on women because, if we are to be completely honest about it, these guys wouldn't stand a snowball's chance in hell of scoring a woman any other way, and would be relegated to camel and goat love, ensuring that the human species would die out as quickly as it had proliferated. There, I said it.

There's a bit about not selling the female slave to foreigners if she doesn't please her master, which is pretty random. But, if he selects this female servant for his son, then he must grant her the rights of a daughter (Ex. 21:9). Well, that is fair enough, as far as it goes. Then, *"If he marries another woman, he must not deprive the first one of her food, clothing and marital rights"* (Ex. 21:10).

Um.. Commandment Seven, anyone...??! Thou shalt not commit adultery (Ex. 20:14)? Recall that little ditty..? Not even a single chapter past laying down his commandments, and God is already completely ignoring them. God makes out that you'll die horribly if you commit this adultery, but then commands that if you do, you're still liable for the wellbeing of your first wife. It's pretty hard to smite someone if they have two wives to maintain, by God's own Law

Addendums. Hmm, I feel a recursive logic loop beginning to form here, so I'll short-circuit it now and leave you to ponder the ramifications of these contradictory commands from on-high. One final addendum of this is that, *"if he does not provide her with these three things, then she is to go free, without any payment of money"* (Ex. 21:11). Well, what kind of compensation is that?! He's screwed around on her, he doesn't provide her with the three basics of her life, so he can just kick her out the door without a shekel to her name? Where's the disincentive?! Ahh, but I've forgotten myself, haven't I; this is biblical times, not the enlightened era in which we live today, and women are essentially chattel. Just another reason why we should throw this book into the bin of human history and focus on what is truly important, like equality regardless of gender, colour or creed.

Personal Injuries

Ah, the part on bodily violations! Let's see what God has in store for us here, shall we? Okay! Right, first up: *"Anyone who strikes a person with a fatal blow is to be put to death"* (Ex. 21:12). Fair enough, in those times, and how at times we wish it was still those times in our times! Then we read, *"However, if it is not done intentionally, but God lets it happen, they are to flee to a place I will designate"* (Ex. 21:14).

Firstly, how would you determine that, "God let it happen"? Will God testify in front of the judges to exonerate the guilty party?

Judges: So it was totes you letting it happen, was it, G..?

G: Yeah, guv: Barry was a prick of a man, and when Shaun snotted him one, he totes deserved it. I mean, I could've softened his fall a bit, but y'know, he was such a prick of a man, so I let that rock split his head like a watermelon.

Judges: Okay, no problemo, he can flee. Soo, do you want us to designate the place to flee to, or is that your call? I'm a little fuzzy on that part of the law.

G: Yeah, that's my call. Let him go to, ooh, China … oh wait, you don't know about them, do you … Russia .. nope, not them, either… damn…. fuck it, let him go back to Egypt, they seem to be short on slaves at the moment, he'll fit right in.

Judges: Sweeeet. Court is adjourned.

See? Madness. As if God would put himself on the witness stand to testify for someone who'd lost his temper and inadvertently killed a guy. Totally unlikely to happen. Then we have, *"If anyone schemes and kills someone deliberately, that person is to be taken from my altar and put to death"* (Ex. 21:15). So, Commandment Six, as it was chiseled. Easy peasy.

"Anyone who attacks their mother or father is to be put to death" (Ex. 21:16). Yeah, there's plenty of parents out there today that wouldn't mind this one still being in vogue. I suppose that's why children are small and cute, so that the temptation to murder them is largely mitigated.

"Anyone who kidnaps someone is to be put to death, whether the victim is sold or is still in the kidnapper's possession" (Ex. 21:17). Well yeah, kidnapping is a terrible thing, I won't deny that fact, and harsh punishments should be applied, but I feel death is a little extreme, especially if it is done to the benefit of the victim, e.g. if it's to remove a "victim" from a physically, mentally or sexually abusive parent, effectively rescuing them from further harm. As always, there is a grey area that must be explored and analyzed before punishments are applied.

"Anyone who curses their mother and father is to be put to death" (Ex. 21:18). Somehow, I don't think we're talking about anything as prosaic as, "Screw you, mum and dad!!", but rather a curse of the more witchcrafty, heartfelt-appeal-to-supernatural-powers variety, designed to create ill health or general hardship to one's parents. It would certainly be overkill (pun intended) to put your teenage offspring to death because they told you to sit on it and rotate; but you'd

rightly toe the line if they were sitting naked in a pentagram at midnight asking the powers of darkness to sodomize you for not letting them listen to their iSheep after 8pm.

Okay, what else? Uhh, if you fight someone and brain them with a rock (or your fist) but they don't die, you won't be held liable, provided they can walk it off after a few days; after some bed rest and the aid of a staff, but you're liable for any loss of wages, apparently. (Ex. 21:18 – 21:19). Ah, okay, *"Anyone who beats their male or female slave with a rod must be punished if the slave dies as a direct result, but they are not to be punished if the slave recovers after a day or two, since the slave is their property"* (Ex. 21:20 – 21:21). Again, if they can walk it off, then there is no comeback for the assault. Charming. I've said it for years; it doesn't matter whether a person is a CEO or a street sweeper, they are still a person and deserving of respect. There are, of course, caveats to that, such as if that person is a thief or a paedophile, in which case they don't count as human and will be treated with the utter contempt they deserve. But for the most part, we're all in this together, so why not respect that and try to get along as best as we are able?

Moving on. Okay, if two guys are fighting and they hit a pregnant woman (it must be some fight!) and it induces labour as a result but no other injury, then the offender is to be fined what the woman's husband requires, so long as the court allows it (Ex. 21:22). But if there is serious injury, you are to, *"take life for life, eye for eye, tooth for tooth, hand for hand, foot for foot, burn for burn, wound for wound, bruise for bruise"* (Ex. 21:23 – 21:25). Covering all the bases, I suppose, but I can't help thinking that, if a pregnant woman is in the middle of a fight between two guys, it's often because there are reasonable doubts over who is the father.

If you hit your slave and they lose an eye, then you have to let 'em go free to compensate for the eye (Ex. 21:26), and the same applies for a tooth (Ex. 21:27). Losing an eye would suck, but there are 32 teeth in your head. Losing one of those would seem to be your easiest ticket to freedom, especially if it saves the agony when those damnable wisdom teeth start punching through your gums, moshing the other teeth around and causing you all sorts of grief.

Okay, if a bull gores someone to death, then you have to stone the thing to death, but you're not allowed to eat the meat, and the owner of the bull can't be held responsible (Ex. 21:28). Buuut, if the bull has a habit of goring people and the owner has been told, but does nothing about it, then the owner joins in the bull's fate (Ex. 21:29). Fair enough, that. A male cow is a bloody great shit of a thing with big horns and a nasty attitude, especially during the breeding season. Anyone stupid enough to go near one of these things deserves everything they get, but yeah, if the owner lets the bugger run free in the streets poking holes in innocent passers-by, then he deserves to have his head caved in with a rock, sure. Buuut, the owner can redeem his life if any sort of payment is demanded by the wronged party. This law applies if the bull gores a son or daughter as well, how nice. If it happens to be a slave of either sex, then there's a fee of thirty shekels in addition to the usual bovine stoning.

Okay, if you dig a hole (or fail to cover one), and an ox or donkey falls into it, you have to pay the owner for the loss, and take the dead animal. Additionally, if your bull kills someone else's bull, you have to sell your bull and divide the money with the other guy, and you have to bifurcate the dead one and share it (Ex. 21:35); buuuut, if your bull has a habit of goring, then you have to pay for the dead bull, but you get to keep the dead bull after. A good way to keep a supply of fresh moople in your diet, that's for sure.

And that's, thankfully, the end of that chapter. I found it about as exciting as any chapter on American Tax Law, so let's hope the next one provides us with some giggles. Onward..!

Exodus 22: God Hates Tea-Leaves, Goat Fanciers

"Hypocrisy is not a way of getting back to the moral high ground. Pretending you're moral, saying you're moral is not the same as acting morally." - Alan Dershowitz

Oh great, more bloody laws and provisos. Well, I suppose the bible has been touted as the go-to book for how to behave, although up until now that guidance hasn't made a lick of sense. The laws outlined in the first part of this chapter, however, I happen to agree with, as it concerns itself with how to deal with that most parasitic and detestable of creatures, the thief. I can only imagine that, if anything should be adhered to in the bible, it should be this part. If nothing else, it would be a fitting deterrent to those who feel they can put their grubby mitts on others' hard-earned possessions. Having lived in a part of the world where burglaries and theft is a nightly occurrence, and the justice system in the land is nothing more than a revolving door and a slap on the hand with a warm lettuce leaf, having some of these ideas enforced with extreme prejudice might actually deter people from taking liberties with your stuff. Those people more removed from Reality (lawyers, politicians, Social Justice Warriors and other people of negligible intelligence) might adopt a live-and-let-live mentality to these miscreants, but I'm willing to bet that they haven't had the sanctity of their home violated with blatant disregard for the home owners. Put bluntly, thieves are the pariahs of society, to be scraped off like a barnacle off a ship's hull, and that will always be the case.

Anyway, rant over, let's get on with these laws and see if we can find something useful in this lot. First up, *"Whoever steals an ox or sheep and slaughters it or sells it must pay back five head of cattle for the ox and four sheep for the sheep"* (Ex. 22:1). That would certainly prevent the casual thief, if this were upheld today, although what you would do with five Playstations and four X-Boxes is anyone's guess. The LAN parties would be pretty sweet, though.

The next one is harsh but, I feel, fair: *"If a thief is caught breaking in at night and is struck a fatal blow, the defender is not guilty of bloodshed; but if it happens after sunrise, then the defender is guilty of bloodshed"* (Ex. 22:2 – 22:3). I can only suppose that the distinction was made so that people couldn't just brain their unwanted daytime visitors with a rock and claim they were thieves breaking in to steal their shit, but for my money it shouldn't matter what time of day it is; the thief is there to steal your stuff, and therefore he suffers the consequences of that choice. As I mentioned before, I live in an area of the world where certain antisocial elements will steal anything that isn't nailed down - often while the owner is at home - and think that they're completely entitled to do so. Sadly, the prevalence of bleeding-heart groups has created a situation where apprehending these antisocial miscreants is treated as a hate crime or, "racist," despite us ALL being members of the human race. It's a very frustrating state of affairs, because as far as I'm concerned, we should *all* be bound by the same laws regardless of colour, creed or culture. If you're human, then the law applies to you, end of story.

Okay, moving on. There's heaps more about your cattle grazing on other peoples' land and burning shit down whether intentional or not, shit that you've borrowed that is then stolen, disputes over ownership, et cetera. I'll leave it to you to peruse in greater detail in your own Good Book (assuming you have one), but it's droll stuff, outlining basic moralistic behaviour that anyone with two brain cells to rub together should be able to understand. In the meantime, let's look for something juicier.

Social Responsibility

Well, there's a few interesting things here, so let's get to it, shall we? Starting with virgins:

"If a man seduces a virgin who is not pledged to be married and sleeps with her, he must pay the bride-price, and she shall be his wife" (Ex. 22:16).

Essentially, you banged it, you bought it. But if the father refuses to hand her over, the guy still has to pay the bride-price. So, the screwing he gets for the screwing he got, but one can't help but wonder what happens to this ex-virgin, considering they usually stone them for being unclean or guilty of provoking it. Whatever.

"Do not allow a sorceress to live" (Ex. 22:18). Well, that was random. How did the author of this book of morals make the mental leap from virgin bride-prices to the slaughter of witches? The two are usually at opposite ends of the Female Spectrum, if all that business about dancing naked around stone formations in the middle of the night has any basis in fact. And what, exactly, is meant by "sorceress" in the biblical scheme of things? A woman, certainly, but doing what? Is she a mixer of herbs, or a fortune teller, or merely a sexy temptress? A quick peek ahead to Deuteronomy (18:9 – 18:14 to be precise) spells it out a little better: If she is sacrificing a son or daughter in a fire, or engaged in divination of sorcery, interpreting omens, doing witchcraft, casting spells, or is a medium/spiritualist who talks to the dead, then you have a sorceress on your hands.

Let's just run through those one more time, shall we?

- Sacrificing a son/daughter: Well, Crazy Old Abe did that to Jacob (Gen. 22);

- Engaging in divination/sorcery: Joseph is guilty of that with his silver cup (Gen. 44);

- Interpreting omens: I'm lookin' at you again, Joey (Gen. 40);

- Doing witchcraft: Moses, that's on you with your water trick (Ex. 14);

- Talking to spirits: Take your pick! Abe, Jacob, Joseph, Moses, all of 'em talking to invisible people. Crazy fuckers..

So according to the listed behaviours, all of the abovementioned biblical figures are guilty of at least one act of sorcery and should have been stoned to death before they could harm anyone. I suppose it comes down to how you interpret it, doesn't it? If you have God pissing in your ear, you can soothsay and omen-read and talk to invisible people; but if you don't then you're a witch and should be killed. I smell the rank odour of Double Standards here. Of course, this is the bible we're talking about, so we should expect many more examples of it before we finish our journey.

Here's one that should be self-explanatory: *"Anyone who has sexual relations with an animal is to be put to death"* (Ex. 22:19). It's not really that hard to fathom, despite the plethora of internet videos proving me otherwise. If you're doing it with a donkey, humping a horse, copulating a camel, grunting a goat, shagging a sheep or goosing a goose, then you're a certified sicko.

"Whoever sacrifices to any god other than the LORD must be destroyed" (Ex. 22:20). Again with the jealous, possessive god thing. But really, it's your own fault, G-man, for creating other gods; if you wanted humanity for yourself only, why create competition for yourself, you big git?

"Do not mistreat or oppress a foreigner, for you were foreigners in Egypt" (Ex. 22:21), which is completely at odds with the Passover caveats of Ex. 12 where meals were refused to foreigners until they'd been genitally mutilated, and being forced to observe your sabbath requirements in Ex. 20; I would say that falls neatly under both categories of Mistreatment and Oppression, wouldn't you agree, readers? I'm sure there are other examples, but these two spring to mind most readily.

Here's a fun one: *"Do not take advantage of the widow or the fatherless. If you do and they cry out to me, I will certainly hear their cry"* (Ex. 22:22). Fair enough, don't be a predatory prick, got it. The next bit is better: *"My anger will be aroused, and I will kill you with the sword; your wives will become widows and your children fatherless"* (Ex. 22:24).

So God will *kill me with the sword*. Will that be in Humanoid form or Burning Bush form, G-man, because I'll need to alter my kata accordingly. Additionally, my *wives* (plural) will be widows, meaning Commandment Seven is being utterly ignored, yet again. I mean, yeah, I get it, there are times when you need to change your laws to suit changing times; but when you change them or just ignore them completely without any acknowledgment or explanation, it's just ridiculous. Letting your peeps have multiple wives, for example, then making a law that forbids adultery, only to talk about multiple wives again as though that law was never made has all the hallmarks of schizophrenia. But then we only have to look back through Genesis to understand God's behaviours in this regard. I'm sure we'll find more as we go along.

Okay, what next? *If you lend money to the needy, don't treat it like a business deal and don't charge interest.* It'd be nice if our banks adhered to that. *"If you take your neighbour's cloak as a pledge, return it by sunset"* (Ex. 22:26). Well, what use is that, if the neighbour hasn't made good on his loan by then, and you just give back your collateral? How daft.

Here's a cool one: *"Do not blaspheme God or curse the ruler of your people"* (Ex. 22:28). Meaning that America, between Clinton and Trump alone, should have about five people left alive, instead of the 330 million it enjoys today. The same goes for Australia, the UK, and just about every country you could name that's had an issue with how their elected leader/s run (or, in some cases, ruin) the country whilst incumbent. The fact that we're all alive today means that we don't have to worry too much about divine retribution anytime soon. *"Do not hold back offerings from your granaries or your vats"* (Ex. 22:29). A big god has a big thirst, so he needs to extort your booze, and your gluten-free bread to wash it down with, for him and all his angel peeps. So don't be a stingy mortal, or he'll zap you.

"You must give me the firstborn of your sons" (Also Ex. 22:29). Because God likes YMCA and the sight of your firstborn son inna skimpy crop top, black leather boy pants and a feather head-dress gets his motor running. *"Do the same with your cattle and your sheep. Let them stay with their mothers for seven days, but give them to me on the eighth day"* (Ex. 22:30). Lamb and baby beef on tap, to put between bits of gluten-free bread obviously. You know, the more we read these conditions, the more we have to conclude that God, whoever he was, was either corporeal at some stage of this meddling with humanity, or that humanity simply believed him to be so, lacking the imagination to fully grasp what non-coporeal meant. Why else would humanity think he would want bread, beef, lamb, boys, and all other manner of things a more incorporeal being would have absolutely no interest in? We are still left with the question of what, or who, this God creature was, and why

he was always interfering with our society. And if our Spaceman Scenario holds any weight, it would stand to reason that, instead of growing and storing the necessary supplies to restock their ship, they would just create an elaborate God myth to convince people to give up their food, wine, etc. without a fight, for the unfulfilled promise of a glorious afterlife. Pretty tight extortion racket, if I do say so myself; no muss, no fuss, people bring their shit to you and expect nothing in return until they die, and then the problem of recompense solves itself.

One last one: *"Do not eat the meat of an animal torn by wild beasts; throw it to the dogs"* (Ex. 22:31). This one, at least, may have some basis in Science. We certainly wouldn't want to get in between an apex predator and its prey, which is fair enough, but I think the law refers to those carcasses that have been accessed by scavengers such as hyenas, vultures, etc. They're not the most hygienic of creatures, and as such would contaminate any meat they chow down on. The Komodo Dragon, in particular, has so many diseases running amok in its mouth that it only has to bite its prey once, then follow it until it succumbs to systemwide toxic shock and dies. This process will take between three and five hours, but the dragon is a patient hunter. After this flood of deadly toxins invades and contaminates the hapless animal, the idea of scavenging any part of it for human consumption is nothing short of a death wish. Presumably this is the reasoning behind this particular law. As for the dogs? Dogs will happily eat each other's shit, so I can't see any lasting problems giving them this type of meat.

Phew, another chapter down! Let's hope it's the last of these bloody law addendums, and return to the dissection of some sort of storyline.

Exodus 23: Oh Goody More Laws, and The Israelite Horde Advances

"It is the habit of every aggressor nation to claim that it is acting on the defensive." -Jawaharlal Nehru.

It had to happen. More bloody addendums. But there are only a few, so we'll run through them briefly before we get to something better later in the chapter.

Laws of Justice and Mercy

Well, that'll be an interesting read, considering the historically bloodthirsty, murderous nature of the line of Abraham. What the hell, let's see if they've learned a few things over the years.

"Do not spread false reports, and don't help a guilty person by being a malicious witness" (Ex. 23:1). Not a bad start, but easier said than done with this mob. Next, *"Do not follow the crowd in doing wrong. When you give testimony in a lawsuit, do not pervert justice by siding with the crowd, and don't show favouritism to a poor person in a lawsuit"* (Ex. 23:2-23:3). Okay, so trying to keep things fair, I get it. Although an angry mob rarely thinks it's in the wrong when it goes on its rampage of civil unrest. To the mob, it's usually some miscarriage of justice that brought them together in the first place, so good luck enforcing that one rationally.

Next, *"If you come across your enemy's ox or donkey wandering off, be sure to return it. And if you see the donkey of someone who hates you fallen down under its load, do not leave it there; be sure you help them with it"* (Ex.23:5). Another fair call, it's not the donkey's fault that it's owned by your dickhead neighbour. Of course, if it's the donkey itself who hates you, then you can sit back and laugh your "ass" off at it… yeah okay that was bad; moving on. *"Don't deny justice to your poor people in a lawsuit"* – another good one, that. Don't put an honest person to death, don't accept bribes, don't oppress a foreigner. Basic morality stuff, really, that anyone with two brain cells to rub together *should* be able to comprehend easily enough. We'll see how many of these they'll remember in later chapters.

Sabbath Laws

More 7th day resting stuff, with a longer period of time for your fields and crops, making sure a field is left unused once every seven years after being used for the first six. And even today, farmers across the world use field rotations to ensure the soil isn't stripped of nutrients, but usually on a four year rotation where they will either leave it fallow or plant lupins on it which are then turned back into the soil to replenish the nitrogen and other trace elements required to grow healthy crops. More crap about seventh day layabouts, and then, *"Do not invoke the names of other gods; do not let them be heard on your lips"* (Ex.23:13). I can't see how it matters one way or the other. If God is everything the devout say he is, then he obviously created these gods himself, so why prevent us from saying their names? And if he did create all those other gods, aren't they, ipso-facto, just an extension of the essence of God himself? If God is so jealous of these other gods, why doesn't he smite the bastards out of existence? Why did he create them at all, if he's going to be a jealous dick about people worshipping them? What a bonehead.

The Three Annual Festivals

Yeah, festival time, everyone loves a festival! It would seem that God wants the Israelites to celebrate three events in particular: the Festival of Unleavened Bread, where they do the seven days of no yeast thing. Fair enough, celebrate the day they were freed and began eating bug shit for forty years; who wouldn't want to celebrate that, right? We also find an interesting bit at the end of this: *"No one is to appear before me empty-handed"* (Ex. 23:15). Another instance of God being corporeal, and extorting some sort of tribute from the worshippers. I mean, really, can't God cook something for himself once in a millennium? Bloody needy god...!

The second festival is the Festival of Harvest, and the third being the Festival if Ingathering, both of which involve food, of course; and commanding that, *"Three times a year all the men are to appear before the Sovereign LORD"* (Ex. 23:17), but imploring them not to offer blood from their sacrifices, or any offering containing yeast. Because, you know, cramps. And then telling them that the fat from these festival offerings *"must not be kept until morning"* (Ex.23:18). Probably because after the last festival, God hit the piss a little too hard and the smell of the fatty leftovers in the morning had God riding the Porcelain Bus, and it won't do to catch your deity kneeling in the privy trench throwing up a lung. Now, some people will swear by a nice, greasy meal after a big night on the sauce, but God isn't one of those people, apparently.

Another example of the extortion of foodstuffs here: *"Bring the best of the firstfruits of your soil to the house of the LORD your God"* (Ex. 23:19), followed incongruously with, *"Do not cook a young goat in its mother's milk."* So even God has some limits on what he considers appropriate. Sure, you can kill and murder and steal and lie and ogle (well, not anymore, of course, because Commandments), but milking your goat so you can cook its kid is crossing some sort of line, apparently. But notwithstanding this oddness, it's obvious that God is keeping these people basically indentured to him and his crew, and making them hand over their best foodstuffs, thereby avoiding having to do it themselves. Maybe as a result of their replicators being offline for whatever reason, or just because they wanted some fresh food every now and again, who knows? All of which indicates that God continues to be corporeal at this stage of the story, and therefore mortal although certainly more technologically advanced compared to us. More on that as we continue the story.

God's Angel to Prepare the Way

In this part of our chapter, we encounter God once again pandering to this mob of whiners, though who he is speaking to is unclear, for it is not mentioned in the usual manner. I'm going to presume he's rapping with Moses again, for the simple reason of him being the major figure in this entire saga. We start off thusly: *"See, I am sending an angel ahead of you to guard you along the way and to the place I have prepared"* (Ex. 23:20). So yeah, great, more wandering, I was hoping we were done with that nonsense. Apparently not. So, the Israelites are told to pay attention to this angel and follow his orders and not to rebel or he'll get all smitey on them; and if they do all that, God promises to, *"be an enemy to your enemies and will oppose those who oppose you"* (Ex. 23:22). So we now have a god who, despite creating the universe and all of humanity, is still playing favourites with one small group of whiners at the expense of the rest of humanity and, indeed, the universe. Sounds legit, not. Let's see how this progresses: *"My angel will go ahead of you and bring you into the land of the Amorites, Hittites, Perizzites, Canaanites, Hivites and Jebusites, and I will wipe them out"* (Ex. 23:23). Well, fuck you and the donkey you rode in on, God. What did these nations ever do to you, to deserve to have genocide visited upon them? You just finished telling your peeps to help their enemies if their donkey runs away or whatever; then you tell 'em you're going to obliterate them and annex their lands! If you want people to live in peace and harmony, then you lead by example, *not* by smiting everyone else out of existence! You are a terrible role model.

Let's see what else we have here. *"Do not bow down before their gods or worship them or follow their practices. You must demolish them and break their sacred stones to pieces"* (Ex. 23:24). More advocating of violence and intolerance, masquerading in the name of peace and love. Isn't religion great? Anyway, there's some more about their food and water being blessed if they toe God's line, and healing them of sickness and them not miscarrying babies, full life spans and other baseless nonsense. Then we get to Ex. 23:27: *"I will send my terror ahead of you and throw into confusion every nation you encounter. I will make all your enemies turn their backs and run."* From the sounds of it, every other nation on the earth at this time is their official enemy. How to win friends and influence people, yeah? Further: *"I will send the hornet ahead of you to drive out the Hivites, Canaanites and Hittites out of your way. But I will not drive them out in a single year, because the land would become desolate and the wild animals too numerous for you"* (Ex. 23:28 – 23:29).

I'm very interested in this "hornet" God has referred to here. Surely, he did not have a single large striped flying insect of the *Vespidae* family buzzing ahead and swooping the hapless land owners and driving them out; that would just be absurd. Something else is meant here, and we know from our own modern military that we name our aircraft after all manner of fauna we consider fearful. The McDonnell Douglas F/A-18 is officially designated the Hornet, for example. Is it more likely that God sent some sort of military aircraft ahead of the Israelites to conduct air strikes against these other tribes? Firing at goat herders with his air-to-ground missiles and scattering the survivors with a pair of M61 Vulcan cannons? It's hard to imagine needing more than one such hornet for the task, with that sort of overkill; talk about swatting a mosquito with a sledge hammer!

And another thing: If God is capable of driving thinking, sentient people from their land and annex it for his chosen peeps, why can't he also protect them from simple wild animals? Has he forgotten how to render them docile with his almighty Will, as he supposedly did for Noah so he could skull-drag them into the ark? Seems to me like this "god" is losing his powers along with his sanity, but that's just my assessment.

Let's continue: *"Little by little I will drive them out before you, until you have increased enough to take possession of the land"* (Ex. 23:30). So now we've come full circle, and the Exodus has become an Invasion; for what else would you call the influx of over six hundred thousand men flooding your lands with an advanced air craft at the van, but a hostile army? If it looks like a duck, and quacks like a duck, et cetera. God then outlines what borders he's going to give to these usurpers, before saying, *"I will give into your hands the people who live in the land, and you will drive them out before you"* (Ex. 23:31). *Again* with the one-verse reversal, G-man? Is it *you* driving the people out, or are the Israelites doing the heavy lifting here? Keep your bloody story straight for at least one friggin' verse, will you?!

Ugh.. what do we have left here? Ah yes, *"Do not make a covenant with them or with their gods,"* and, *"Do not let them live in your land or they will*

190

cause you to sin against me, because the worship of their gods will certainly be a snare to you" (Ex. 23:32 – 23:33). Well, of course he's going to say that. When you're controlling, unforgiving, smitey, insanely jealous and prone to vicious psychopathic episodes, you're not going to want your peeps engaging in the worship of other, more mentally-stable gods; so you do the only thing you can in this position, which is to segregate them from any gods more beneficent than you (in his case, *all* of 'em) and ensure this segregation by forbidding any efforts towards peaceful cohabitation and eliminating all other religions and their followers. By these simple measures, God may have liberated the Israelites from the Egyptians, but they're still very much a hostage to an insane, violent god. I can't see this ending well.

Exodus 24: God Holds A Dinner Party

"At a formal dinner party, the person nearest death should always be seated closest to the bathroom." - George Carlin.

We begin this chapter with God inviting Mose and the elders to an impromptu dinner party. To be specific: *"The LORD said to Moses, 'Come up to the LORD, you and Aaron, Nadab and Ahibu, and seventy of the elders of Israel. You are to worship at a distance, but Moses alone is to approach the LORD; the others must not come near. And the people may not come up with him.'"* (Ex. 24:1 – 24:2). It's funny when you realize that God's feeding these people with their own food that they've offered up to him as offerings. And if we cast our mind back to Chapter 6, we'll remember that Nahab and Abihu were Aaron's older two brats. It kinda makes you wonder why Mose didn't have his own two kids in this purple circle, but I guess he had his reasons at the time. Anyway, after securing the blind obeisance of the masses and writing everything G-man told him, he, *"got up early the next morning and built an altar at the foot of the mountain and set up twelve stone pillars representing the twelve tribes of Israel"* (Ex. 24:4).

This is a pretty labour-intensive activity for an octogenarian to be attempting by himself. Don't get me wrong, there are some pretty active pensioners about, even today: my own father once helped manhandle three pallets of paving bricks at the tender age of 83, despite repeated requests from his prodigal son to, "geroff out of it and sit down, ya bugger..!" and the buyers of said pavers, less than half his age, gob-smacked at his stamina. The twelve tribes of Israel refers to the twelve sons of Jacob/Israel/whatever, so that explains that with a minimum of fuss.

Anyway, once these stone altars and pillars have been built, *then* he sends young Israelite men off to do the burnt offerings and slaughter young bulls. The brainless bugger could have used their strength for the rocks, but nooo, burn this shit and kill some cows. Well done. Mose then collected half of the blood and put it into bowls, and the other half he splashed against the altar he'd built (Ex. 24:6). I suppose he just cupped his hands for the other half, whatever. Once this was done, he grabbed his handy-dandy note book and read out everything he'd scribbled to the people, who responded, *"We will do everything the LORD has said; we will obey"* (Ex. 24:7). Trouble is, seeing as Moses is the only person God's talking to at the moment, it's pretty hard to verify any of the things he's written in his notebook, isn't it? Having been commanded to remain at a distance, it's not like they can wander up to God and ask, "Hey, G-man, did you *really* say that? I mean, it doesn't make a lot of sense when you think about it, and…" *ZAP!!!*

And there's that Deterrent™, of course. Perhaps Commandment Eleven should have been, "Thou Shalt Not Think."

But I digress, as usual. Once the peeps have indicated their blind obeisance, Mose grabs the bowls of blood and *"sprinkled it on the people and said, 'This is the blood of the covenant that the LORD has made with you in accordance with all these words.'"* (Ex. 24:8). Now, it could just be me, but any ritual that requires its advocates to be splashed in blood isn't the kind of social group I want to be a part of, thank you very much. It bears a striking resemblance to the kinds of rituals the guy Downstairs prefers, despite there not being any mention of the horny bastard as yet. No matter, I suppose he'll rock up eventually; but it is interesting how your typical Sunday doorknockers omit these nasty bits when proselytizing their beliefs at you. Next time you encounter one of these misguided souls, ask them if they still re-enact the blood covenant; then watch their stares change from blank to horror as you describe what's in their own book. Fun times.

After he'd had his fun painting his peeps red, Moses, Aaron, Nadab and Abihu and the seventy elders, *"went up and saw the God of Israel"* (Ex. 24:10). Actually saw the mad bugger with their eyes, for what other interpretation could you draw from that? They also describe walking on, *"something like a pavement made of lapis lazuli, as bright blue as the sky"* (Ex. 24:10). Now, if God was, indeed, some advanced being coming down to earth and landing a ship on the top of the mountain, this is easily explained as the floor of the ship. We know from all of our sci-fi movies and television series that blues figure quite prominently and are regarded in our minds as "more advanced" somehow; from lighting to workstations and panels, buttons, weapons, everything. Don't ask me why, it just is. Perhaps, if these events were the result of an extraterrestrial meeting, it has shaped our bias toward this colour in our ancestral memory. Those of you who have read Douglas Adams' Hitchhiker's Guide series will recall with fondness the beings described as, "a hyper-intelligent shade of blue;" and how the Vogons, as mere menial, bureaucratic dullards, hulked about in ugly yellow construction ships. Those who subscribe to such things as "auras" and kirlian photography will rave about how our baser emotions reside in the lower end of the visible spectrum (reds, oranges) whereas the nobler attributes of mental acuity and spiritual enlightenment are often associated with blues and purples. Even today, bishops and senior bishops will wear purple to indicate their elevated position within their church, along with gold thread which, as we know, is a precious metal and as such has been usurped along with these higher colours to prove their alleged superiority over the rabble of humanity. It's a shame it didn't stop them succumbing to their baser urges concerning the choir boys, but we'll deal with that another time (and I'm not talking about them playing, "Run to Paradise" repeatedly on the church organ).

Back to the narrative. *"God did not raise his hand against these leaders of the Israelites; they saw God, and they ate and drank"* (Ex. 24:11). And why would he, exactly? It was God himself who told Mose to bring all these people up for the dinner party right at the start of the chapter; it would be Bad Form indeed to then smite them during the main course, ensuring dismal attendance numbers at any subsequent dinner parties. It also intrigues me how these guys could have looked upon this "God" without suffering dire consequences. We are told throughout the bible that gazing upon God's face will get you dead, either by smiting or by salt pillar or some other nasty development; so how did these buggers kick back at God's barbeque and eat and drink with the big guy and not end up as smoking piles of ash? Surely the countenance of God – this supposedly benevolent, kind, caring God of Man – isn't such a terrible thing to behold? Are we talking "The Elephant Man" deformity here, or what? It could very well explain why some people worship Ganesh, come to think of it …

please excuse that quick jump to another pantheon, but it did beg the question.

Anyway, while they're enjoying this divine repast with the big guy, he apparently says to Moses, *"Come up to me on the mountain and stay here, and I will give you the tablets of stone with the law and commandments I have written for their instruction"* (Ex. 24:12). Riiight, you're going to give an octogenarian two massive stone slabs to lug back down the mountain all by himself, are you? What a dick move, G-man, why don't you just give the fucker a heart attack now and be done with it? Ugh. The next verse is interesting, though: *"Then Moses set out with Joshua his aide, and Moses went up on the Mountain of God"* (Ex. 24:13). Well, okay, two people hoofed it up the mountain, not one. Mose apparently told the gathering to wait for them, leaving Aaron and Hur to resolve any disputes while they're gone. Then they started climbing, whereupon cloud apparently covered the mountaintop.

Then we're told, *"For six days the cloud covered the mountain, and on the seventh day the LORD called to Moses from within the cloud"* (Ex. 24:16). I hope Mose packed a sandwich or four and took a waterbag, or there might not have been much left of him by Day Seven. And what a dick God is for making him wait a week until he rocked up for the pow-wow, despite it being God's invitation in the first place. I know that if I was kept waiting for a week for someone to rock up with no food, water or excuse for tardiness, I'd be royally pissed. Mind you, I'd have probably pissed off as soon as biological needs such as hunger and thirst demanded my attention more than some fickle, tardy god. Of course, this wait is just another opportunity to remind everyone of this seven-day rubbish, which happens to be one of the principle tenets in Sabbatarianism and lead to the subsequent founding of the 7th Day Adventist church/cult/splinter group of religious worship (circle applicable). Moses, for his part, *"stayed on the mountain forty days and forty nights"* (Ex. 24:18); whether that was due to him waiting for God to chisel out the stone tablets, or more likely chisel them out himself because he's made it up as he goes along with some help from astronomical anomalies and perhaps a great deal of hallucinogenic herbs mixed in with the Israelites' bugshit, or even because he wanted to match Noah's 40-day ark thingy. Well, the rainy bit anyway.

Exodus 25: God Acts like a Fucking Diva

"I'd love to be a diva. But I'd then have to send so many apology notes for my abhorrent behaviour." - *Amy Adams.*

It's never a good thing when God starts making worldly demands of you, especially when God supposedly created everything and therefore can create anything (or anyone) he damn well pleases. If your god ever demands corporeal things from you, perhaps take a moment and ask why he would even need it.

Offerings for the Tabernacle

We start off by God telling Moses to, *"Tell the Israelites to bring me an offering. You are to receive the offering for me from everyone whose heart prompts them to give"* (Ex. 25:1). So, God isn't going to receive these things personally, it will be Moses. Interesting. The list of things God apparently wants is quite impressive:

Gold, silver and bronze;

Blue, purple and scarlet yarn and fine linen;

Goat hair;

Ram skins dyed red and durable leather;

Acacia wood;

Olive oil for light;

Spices for anointing oil and fragrant incense;

Onyx stones and other gems (to be mounted on an ephod and breastpiece, apparently).

Sounds like quite a haul, and still no reason why God couldn't just create all of this with a snap of his fingers, instead taking the stuff from his followers like an extortionist. But then, God isn't getting this stuff, is he? Moses is collecting all this for some purpose; let's see what it is.

God then commands the Israelites to, *"make a sanctuary for me, and I will dwell among them. Make this tabernacle and all its furnishings exactly like the pattern I will show you"* (Ex. 25:8 – 25:9). Ahh, so God wants to go Glamping, huh? It's the only way to rationalize this: how else would God deign to leave the advanced, comfortable surrounds of his ship to slum it with a bunch of smelly, primitive goat herders? Ridiculous!

The Ark

What, another one?! But no, this isn't some mere wooden boat to stuff animals in and float about for months on end. This is, if I'm reading this right, the instructions for the building of the Ark of the Covenant, that mystical Indiana Jones box of Smitey Badness that kills all those Nazis trying to control it to win their war effort, those silly sausages!

Now, as per usual and just like my first offering on Genesis, I have taken the time to read each entire bible chapter to get a feel of the overall picture before writing my interpretations based on the world we know today, by combining rational thought, common sense and logical reasoning to dig up those little diamonds of interest out of the coal dust of superstition. So, what do we make of this ark pattern? Let's peruse Ex. 25:10 – 25:22 and see:

Make an ark of acacia wood two and a half cubits long, and one and a half cubits wide as well as high;

Overlay it with pure gold inside and out, with a gold molding around it;

Cast four gold rings attached to each of its four feet;

Make poles of acacia wood overlaid with gold, inserting these into the rings to carry the ark. The poles are to remain in the rings at all times;

Put the stone tablets into the ark;

Make an atonement cover of pure gold for the ark, with two cherubim of hammered gold at each end, facing each other with their wings spreading up and out over the cover;

Put the lid on;

And I'll "meet" you above the cover of the ark where the cherubim's wings meet, to give you commands and shit.

So we have a chest of wood, covered with gold with some goodies inside, which must not be touched, but can be used to talk to God. Sounds to me like we've just made ourselves some sort of transceiver device. We know that gold is an extremely good electrical conductor, and that acacia wood is a very good electrical insulator. It wouldn't surprise me in the slightest if we haven't just gone and built ourselves some sort of ancient capacitor, capable of storing large electrical voltages, like a primitive battery of sorts, much like a Leyden jar. We have a couple of wooden poles so we don't touch the thing (along with being told God will smite us if we touch it), and some fancy cherub work on top fashioned in a particular way. Lining the inside and outside of the wooden box with gold, with an acacia wood insulator, would be capable of holding quite the electrical charge, such that anyone earthing the thing would get one hell of a boot. This is borne out by flicking ahead to 2 Samuel 6:7, where some dude by the name of Uzzah reached out to steady the ark during its trip to Jerusalem, whereby "God" immediately struck Uzzah dead for his "irreverent act." In reality, it's most likely that Uzzah's steadying hand inadvertently joined the inner and outer gold linings of the ark, punching several thousand volts through his body and welding his balls to the sand.

Intrigued at what sort of voltages we're looking at here, I dove headlong into the World of Wiki to get some hard Math. Now remember, this ark was built ostensibly to contain two large stone tablets, a jar full of bugshit and some other mystical relic-type things, so the wood thickness would have to be substantial; let's say about an inch thick for the sake of argument. We then find the relative permittivity of acacia wood (about 5.0) which is also known as its Dielectric Constant, or in layman's terms how well it acts as an electrically-insulating material. We then find the Capacitance of our ark, using the formula C = εr (A/4πd), where:

C = Capacitance measured in farads;

εr = Relative Permittivity of the insulator;

π = Pi;

d = distance between plates

Now, if we put in our variables of 5.0 for the relative permittivity of acacia wood, with a one inch thickness between plates that are essentially 4.5 cubits long (three sides, 1.5 cubits wide) by 2.5 cubits wide (the longer sides) plus the area of the two end panels, we end up with a box with the potential to store up to 150,000 volts, and about 63 joules of electrical energy. To put this into some perspective, between 10-200 joules is in the "Could Kill You" range of electrical dangerousness, and over 200 is in the "Will Kill You" range. Your garden-variety taser will give you between 1/3 and 2 joules per zapping, to give those who've experienced this a better idea of the numbers we're dealing with here. It's little wonder this box was designed to be carried with wooden poles! It's also amusing to consider that we have a group of refugees utilizing electrical energy and smelting gold at an advanced level for the purpose of being able to communicate with a superior being, but who are still using flint knives to hack at each other's genitalia. Or am I the only one seeing a blatant paradox here?

I'm also drawn back to the Netflix series of The Pyramid Code, where the construction of the pyramids themselves (essentially, granite inner with a limestone outer) are now suspected of being giant electrical generation facilities, and not burial tombs as hitherto claimed. With all the other mysteries and reasons surrounding their construction, who can really tell whether or not the Israelites were using some advanced knowledge to communicate with a being not of this planet? Stranger things have occurred, and when you consider we live in a universe where there was a Trump president, we simply have to concede that even the most outrageous of theories is, indeed, possible.

The Table

Here we have a similar intricately described pattern as the ark, but for a table measuring 2 cubits long, a cubit wide and 1.5 cubits high, with the same overlaying of gold and rings of gold on the legs and so on. I'm not entirely sure that this is to create an electric table, but in some ways it's a shame they didn't make God a chair to match the rest of the furniture. It could have saved us all a great deal of death, murder and misery over the last few thousand years, that's for sure. Oh, and God also wants all the plates and dishes and whatnot made of pure gold, the prima donna. Oh, and God also says, *"Put the bread of the Presence on this table to be before me at all times"* (Ex. 25:30). I suppose it's a bit like leaving milk and cookies for Santa, but in bread form, or he won't bless you with his presents. In this case, there were apparently not one, but twelve breads or cakes left on this table in case God decided to pop in for a quick visit and was hungry. These cakes/breads were left on the table for a week and replaced with fresh loaves every sabbath (despite that pesky thing earlier forbidding them to work on the sabbath; apparently, baking bread for God's bread table is one of his caveats).

The Lampstand

A god needs light to eat by, after all, or his all-seeing mightiness might eat the tablecloth by mistake. This, too, was to be made out of pure gold, and with a level of detail to make the average OCD person feel like they're not trying hard enough. With six branches/arms, and three cups shaped like almond flowers on each arm, with four more cups on the stand itself with buds and blossoms and all sorts of shit, all hammered out of gold and in one piece with the lampstand, with pure gold wick trimmers and trays to boot.

It makes Ozzy Osbourne's demand for one thousand brown M&M's to fill a brandy glass at 3am sound totally reasonable by comparison. I wonder if Mose had to kill the goldsmith and his son with their own sandals?

And really, when we look at all these things as a whole, do we really want to go worshipping a god so utterly cruel and materialistic that he makes the most self-centered diva seem like an austere minimalist, especially when he could make these items himself with far less effort? Additionally, are we to add goldsmithing to Moses' growing resume of talents, including stonemasonry, public speaking, law giving, conjuring and propheteering? Either way you look at it, someone is being taken for a ride, and I strongly suspect it's the uneducated masses gathered at the foot of Mount Sinai.

For more detailed specifications on building these tables and arks and lampshades, feel free to peruse a bible at your leisure, because unless you're going to actually build them, it's just so much needless filler that detracts from what little narrative there is at the moment. Let us move on and leave our diva deity to his gold trappings for now.

Exodus 26: The Tabernacle, An Ikea Original

"My camping days are over, but I might consider glamping." -Christine Feehan.

In this chapter, we are treated not only to how God wants his digs set up for all his gold shit, but what it's made of and where everything goes. The items, requirements, measurements, fittings, curtains, beams, struts, openings, bases, rods, rings, loops and so on are all contained in the chapter, so feel free to boggle at the sheer complexity in your own time. Below is a short list of the components Moses has to scab up for this tabernacle:

10 curtains of fine linen, 28 cubits x 4 cubits;

50 gold clasps for the 50 loops in the curtains;

11 curtains of goat hair, 30 cubits by 4 cubits;

50 bronze clasps for same, for 50 loops;

Ram skins, dyed red, to cover this lot;

A further covering of, "other durable leather";

Acacia framework, 10 cubits x 1.5 cubits;

40 frames for the north and south ends;

80 silver bases for these frames;

6 frames for the west, and 2 for the far corner;

16 further silver bases for these frames;

Gold overlay for all these frames;

15 acacia crossbars with gold overlay and rings;

And So On. It's quite elaborate.

The big takeaway from this chapter, however, is in Ex. 26:30: *"Set up the tabernacle according to the plan shown you on the mountain."* Not given. Shown.

We have to remind ourselves at this point that Moses is well into his eighties when he is given all these things to do, which must be made to exacting measurements and built in extremely specific ways, and he's doing it from *memory*?! That's a pretty risky move when you're dealing with a psychopathic god on a hair-trigger. It is further claimed by biblical scholars that Moses built this tabernacle himself, although it does say in Ex. 26:1 that, "a skilled worker" could be used to weave the cherubim images into the ten curtains God initially demands of Mose. I guess embroidery wasn't on his talent list, because Ex. 26:36 also refers to sub-contracting this work out for the tent flaps at the front. He seems to have the goldsmithing, tanning, dyeing, silver-working, sewing, bronzeworking and carpentry under control, however. Again, it would be so much easier for God to just snap his fingers and create all this rubbish for himself, if he's going to be a pedantic prima donna about it. To entrust it all to the memory on an octogenarian is just asking for trouble if you ask me, unless God was pissing in Moses' ear constantly during the manufacturing phase to ensure the correct dimensions.

And why would God want, or even need, a structure of this complexity? We can explain to some degree the meticulousness of the ark's dimensions, in that it would have to reach a certain voltage, store a certain power level, and the top's precision of the angels' wings and whatnot could perhaps tune that power to a frequency God can use to communicate with his terrestrial playthings; particularly when the onyx is taken into consideration, the precious stone being a cryptocrystalline form of quartz and as such could have been used to establish a base frequency for the ark. But why such exacting dimensions for the tent? Ostensibly we are told it is to house the ark, table, and lampstand of the Covenant, to serve as some sort of holy place for these items; the first structure of its kind mentioned in the bible beyond stone altars for the worship of these three things, something like a church if you will, and yet mobile enough to rip down and take to wherever the Israelites happen to be invading at the time. It sounds like a whole lot of busy-work going on to keep the Israelites occupied instead of sitting around questioning why they're doing all this for an allegedly all-powerful god.

Going back to our Spaceman Scenario, we can surmise that Team Leader Yahweh (if that's who it is, of course, barring him being usurped or institutionalized as suspected in earlier bible passages) has his ship in a stable orbit of the planet – most likely a geostationary one – and lacking any teleportation capabilities, must now travel down to the planet in a shuttle, thereby explaining the whole "descending in fire" thing on the mountain. Given that he's not going to make this trip for a five minute conversation with Mose and his peeps, it's logical to assume that God is making sure that, if he's to spend any length of time on the planet, he's going to spend it in luxury, thankyou very much. And so he shows Moses all the things he's to build – nothing like verbal instructions to create quality infrastructure! – and thus ensures that he has a nice lush tent to live in, with food always on the table ready to eat. It's what I would do if I were lording it over a bunch of half-baked simians. Why else would the Israelites go to such great lengths if they didn't think it would serve a practical purpose, i.e. to accommodate a living, breathing, corporeal "god" during his stay on the planet surface? They got the posh linen walls happening on the inside, the rugged leather walls on the outside, and a nice lining of goat hair to insulate the inside of the tent from the heat and cold respectively. I suppose an argument could be made for sheepskins for the middle layer, until you realize the wool would quickly fill up with desert sand, whereas the goat hair would preclude that buildup. You could ask why God wouldn't just hang out in the shuttle craft he came down in, but if this is indeed the case, it wouldn't do to have your acolytes getting too much exposure to advanced technology. Think of it as one of those, "Prime Directive" things Starfleet insists its starship captains obey at all costs, despite Yahweh making a right-royal botch of the whole affair when he manipulated the DNA of an indigenous primate species for his own twisted amusement.

Relax, things can only get better, right..?

Exodus 27: God's Weber and Outdoor Living

"Barbecue may not be the road to world peace, but it's a start." -Anthony Bourdain

Not content with hanging about in a linen-and-goat-hair tent, God now wants a nice outdoor area to entertain his chosen peeps. Whether he means Mose and the Elders, or his angels/crew members is anyone's guess; but you can't go on a glamping trip without a nice outdoor area to sit about in, and a barbeque to cremate yourself a nice slab of cow/lamb/goat/whatever. So in addition to the myriad complex instructions he gave to Moses in regard to the tent and the ark and the table and the lamp, God now outlines his outdoor living requirements.

God's Weber – er, Altar

As far as barbecues go, this is one righteous mofo. God's instructions are, *"Build an altar of acacia wood, three cubits high; it is to be square, five cubits long and five cubits wide"* (Ex. 27:1). If we maintain the cubit conversion from my Noah's Ark assessment (i.e. 1 cubit == 45.72cm), this will make this Altarcue 1.37m high, and 2.28m square. So it's *big*. Further: *"Make a horn at each of the four corners, so that the horns and the altar are of one piece, and overlay the altar with bronze"* (Ex. 27:2). Now, given that ancient Bronze was most likely an alloy of Copper and Tin, the closest match I could find is Colphos 90 (an alloy of Copper with approximately 12% Tin).

Now I'm going to give Mose some credit here, and assume he can create sheets of bronze of a uniform 3mm thickness for this altar. If we assume he covers all the surfaces and essentially ends up with a hollow bronze cube (as mentioned further down in Ex. 26:8) with an acacia wood support frame, we'll end up with:

4 sheets of 1.37m x 2.28m, 3mm thick; and

2 sheets 2.28m x 2.28m, 3mm thick (yes, a lot of the top sheet will be missing, but this will be made up with the bronze grating, tools, fire pan and other accessories);

which gives us a weight in bronze overlay alone of 614.4kg. So it's also *heavy*. If we were to increase the thickness of the bronze by a single millimetre, the weight of overlay increases to 819.19kg. And this bloody thing is supposed to be *portable!* If we also factor in the appreciable weight of the acacia wood, you'd be looking at an overall weight approaching one tonne, just so God can have a barbeque when he deigns to visit! Talk about overkill.

God's Courtyard

Now God turns his attention to his outdoor entertainment area. In this, he has demanded an area 100 cubits long and 50 cubits wide, the walls of which are to be finely twisted linen (again, God lets Mose divvy out the work to an embroiderer). There are other bits about the courtyard door (also embroidered linen) and that all the other accoutrements such as tent pegs to be made of bronze, but I'm sure you can read all that for yourself at your leisure.

Oil for the Lampstand

A simple request for this one. God merely wants a constant supply of, *"clear oil pressed from olives for the light so that the lamps may be kept burning"* (Ex. 27:20). Further instructions are such that Aaron and his sons are to, *"keep the lamps burning before the LORD from evening until morning. This is to be a lasting ordinance among the Israelites for generations to come"* (Ex. 27:21). Well, assuming this to be true, where are these descendants of Aaron today, and why haven't they been doing their bloody job?

According to an article written by Peter Goodspeed, outlining a genealogy thesis by one Dr. Karl Skorecki of the University of Toronto, the genetic markers of today's Cohanim – Jewish priests – were traced back using the non-coding DNA on the Y-chromosomes of their ancestry, all the way back to, apparently, Aaron, some three and a half thousand years ago when the events of Exodus were supposed to have occurred. All well and good ... until you understand that Judaism is traditionally matrilineal in nature. The line would continue only if every single dude had a Jewish mother. That is, of course, according to the tenets of the

Jewish religion, and nothing to do with simple genetics; but if they're going to claim a thing based on religious principles, they'll just have to play to the rules they've laid down for themselves, yes? So a single non-Jewish mother anywhere in the ancestry would therefore break that line of Jewishness and end the fabled line of Aaron. Neat-o!

Let us continue, and discover what other nice goodies Moses can extort from these hapless Israelites in the name of Team Leader Yahweh.

Exodus 28: Clothes Maketh the Priest

"One person's religion is another person's cult." -
Philip Seymour Hoffman.

This chapter of Exodus concerns itself wholly
and solely with what God's priests are to wear
to distinguish themselves from the rest of the
Israelite rabble, and is predictably as boring as
batshit. But as always, the boring stuff needs to
be covered for the sake of completeness, so that
I can honestly say that every part of Exodus has
been read and considered using modern-day
critical thinking. Still, we might find a hidden
nugget or two to chew on, so get your sweet-
and-sour sauce ready and we'll push on.

The Priestly Garments

First up, God commands, *"Have Aaron your*
brother brought to you from among the Israelites,
along with this sons Nadab and Abihu, Eleazar and
Ithamar, so they may serve me as priests" (Ex.
28:1). Basically, setting up Moses' brother and
all his sons as the high priests in this Praise God
business he's got going on. It's not normally
prudent to mix family and business, but if you
were elevated to a position by an advanced
being, wouldn't you want to drag your homies
along for the ride? Of course you would, except
for those family members you hate, naturally.

So the "priestly garments" are commanded to
be made of the finest linen, crafted by skilled

hands (more outsourcing), and are to comprise of a breastpiece, an ephod (some embarrassing cross between an apron and a dress), a robe, a woven tunic, a turban and a sash. These items were to be made using gold, and blue, purple and scarlet yarn, and fine linen. Only the best materials for those worthy pole turtles!

The Ephod

A smaller paragraph here outlining how to make this apron-dress thing, with dimensions and lengths and materials and whatnot. There are also two stones of onyx on this thing, engraved with the names of the twelve tribes of Israel, six per stone, engraved, *"the way a gem cutter engraves a seal"* (Ex. 28:11). So, we also have gem cutters among the Israelites. Not that this is impossible, really: the art of Lapidary has been around for about a million years, when man first realized you could scratch a soft rock with a hard one. So that, by 3000 BCE, the art had advanced to quite a significant degree. My problem with this passage is that gem cutting would require access to precious gems, which is something you wouldn't readily associate with a group of fugitive Israelite slaves who're more renowned for herding goats and breeding sheep than they are for the gem crafting arts, and that's given that they raped the Egyptians of all the gold and jewelry before they ran off. But then, those gems would already have been cut and shaped, and not the raw gems you'd need to create an original piece. Of course, they could have found some blank onyx stones and hacked a few names into them, but I wouldn't call that "gem cutting" any more than I'd call spray-painted graffiti tags, "art."

But I digress. These stones were to be fixed onto the shoulders of this ephod as memorial stones, so that the lineage is honoured or some such. Then God wants some gold chains made to resemble rope, with some filigree settings to pin it to, in an attempt to bling up his priestly peeps.

The BreastPiece of Decision (+2 Int, -2 Dex)

Next up, God instructs, *"Fashion a breastpiece for making decisions – the work of skilled hands"* (Ex. 28:15). Because you can hardly be expected to make decisions if you don't have the right breastpiece. Lamb roast for dinner, or pork? Coco Pops for breakfast, or toast and vegemite? Smite the Canaanites, or the Jebusites? Without your Ornate Breastpiece of Decision +2, you're screwed. So, this thing is outlined as, "a span" both long and wide, with rows of pretty gems affixed to it, everything from agate to turquoise. Additionally, it was to have twelve stones on it, each with a name of one of the twelve tribes, with more gold rope and links to join this breastpiece to the ephod. Finally, we read: *"Also put the Urim and Thummim in the breastpiece, so they may be over Aaron's heart whenever he enters the presence of the LORD"* (Ex. 28:30).

What are the Urim and Thummim, I hear you ask? Well, they were two stones, one light and one dark, ostensibly so that the priest could get yes/no answers from God. This is interesting to me because such things fall within the realm of Divination (Cleromancy, to be precise), which is a priestly form of witchcraft/sorcery, and yet Ex. 22:18 clearly tells us, *"Do not allow a sorceress to live."* I guess they mean to kill only females, but why should they be stoned for performing the same divination rituals as men? Is it the sorcery they object to, or the gender? Another attempt to keep control over mystical matters and oppress half the population? It astounds me that so many women are willingly bound to the tenets of the bible, when it's so blatantly misogynistic. We're talking about openly submitting to a God who still hasn't gotten over that whole Applegate saga and is continually hating on women forever after for this one act of defiance, or more likely they're submitting to a fiction authored over the ages by misogynistic men to keep women under the thumb, under the guise of Religion. Whichever way you look at it, it speaks volumes about both sides of this equation; and those women who embrace the bible as the absolute truth should really start to question what that book is telling them about their worth in society, and whether that "truth" holds true today. I guarantee you that it does not. So if you find yourself in that situation, and you've managed to read this far without your mind baulking at the heresy, think at least on this, and free yourself of the hate-filled, guilt-laden poison the bible has burdened your mind with for far too long. You owe it to yourself, if nobody else.

The Priestly Grundies, and the rest of it

Just a couple more items of interest here, namely making the robe of the ephod entirely of blue cloth with a hole for the head (because God is a freakin' bower bird and Aaron needs to see where he's going), and interestingly, to *"make pomegranates of blue, purple and scarlet yarn around the hem of the robe, with gold bells between them"* (Ex. 28:33). Odd, but hey, we'll see where he goes with this. Pomegranates have always been revered for their lifegiving health benefits, and is classed as a superfood packed with antioxidants and anti-inflammatory properties; I don't know how much benefit a yarn one will give, though. Next verse: *"Aaron must wear it when he ministers. The sound of the bells will be heard when he enters the Holy Place before the LORD and when he comes out, so that he will not die"* (Ex. 28:35).

So that he will not die..?! Is God such a highly-strung, unpredictable git (or hard of hearing) that he has to put a frickin' bell on his senior priest (Apologies to Dr. Evil..!) to stop him accidentally smiting the poor bastard? Or is the arrangement of yarn balls and gold bells on the ephod, along with the stones, gems, gold and other items, part of some static earthing garment preventing Aaron from being fried by the ark? I'm not sure how the bells/yarnball combo would achieve that; perhaps greater minds than my own can nut it out, given the parameters of previous items and suppositions. Next on the ensemble is a nice turban with a big golden plate with, "HOLY TO THE LORD" engraved on it, which sits on Aaron's forehead when he wears this turban. Supposedly, this is to allow Aaron to, *"bear the guilt involved in the sacred gifts the Israelites consecrate,"* (Ex. 28:38) whatever the hell that means, and would be on Aaron's noggin constantly so that these offerings would be, *"acceptable to the LORD."*

Sigh.

What else..? Some rubbish about sashes and tunics and caps and what not, to be given to Aaron's sons to make them feel superior to everyone else. Then there's some anointing and consecrating going on to make it all official. Then we read, *"Make linen undergarments as a covering for the body, reaching from the waist to the thigh. Aaron and his sons must wear them whenever they enter the tent of meeting or approach the altar to minister in the Holy Place, so that they may not incur guilt and die"* Ex. 28:42 – 28:43). In other words, Aaron and his brats get undies to wear because God doesn't want to see their meat-and-two-veg, and will kill them if he has to deal with that shit. I can hardly see Aaron and his sons dying of guilt, despite some people today claiming to have died of embarrassment; albeit in a figurative sense rather than a literal one.

And that's the end of that chapter. Neeext!

Exodus 29: Bloodied Clothes Maketh the Man

"It is an interesting question how far men would retain their relative rank if they were divested of their clothes." -Henry David Thoreau.

This chapter of Exodus outlines the consecration of God's priests and what rituals and nonsense is required to enter God's Purple Circle, and is just as boring as the last chapter. But we'll see what it has to offer anyway, shall we?

Consecration of the Priests

We've heard in previous chapters of God's command to get Moses' peeps consecrated and whatnot but, until now, no details on how this was achieved was forthcoming. First up is the procuring of one bull and two rams, *"without defect,"* along with a whole bunch of loaves made without yeast (because of God's IBS), which were then put in a basket and presented along with the animals.

Following this, Aaron and his brats get treated to a wash, with actual water. Certainly, this is a mark of extravagance in a desert environment with nothing but sand to bathe in; after which, they all get dressed up in their new threads, at which point Aaron was anointed by pouring oil on his head. Anyone got a match, perchance..?

Next up, the bull is dragged in and Aaron and his sons put their hands on its head before it is slaughtered, *"in the LORD's presence."* This is followed by smearing some of the bull's blood on the horns of the altar, *"with your finger,"* then pouring the rest of the blood at the base of the altar (Ex. 29:11 – 29:12).

I don't know about you, loyal readers, but this is sounding more like a satanic cult than it does a religion. Killing innocent creatures and then plastering the landscape with their blood isn't exactly the happy-clapping image we're used to in today's religions, although the mindlessness of the worshippers remains largely unchanged. Further to this: *"Then take all the fat on the internal organs, the long lobe of the liver, and both kidneys with the fat on them, and burn them on the altar"* (Ex. 29:13). It's bad enough that we have a dead cow on our hands, let alone eviscerating it wholesale and burning its organs. What issue God would have against viscera is uncertain, unless he dropped in on the Scots and he was treated to a holy haggis. An experience like that would make anybody want to cremate organs to prevent such a thing being made ever again. And why pick on the long lobe, whatever that entails, and how did they come about with names for the separate parts of that organ? As far as hepatic etymology is concerned, it wasn't until 1957 when French surgeon Claude Couinaud introduced the idea of eight distinct liver nodes or "segments," so who was pissing in Moses' ear about there being distinct parts of a slimy, squishy brown organ with no immediately obvious function? The idea for this segmentation of the liver would not have occurred naturally to a goat-herding people, so we need to consider that this information was given to them from a more advanced source. As we know from Jacob's experiments with striped sticks to screw Laban, literally, out of his pure sheep, the Scientific Method inherent in the Hebrew people was primitive at best; it would be almost impossible to evolve that method in such a short period of time as to start naming the different structures in a given organ. Even though the Egyptians were at that stage adept at their mummification techniques, there is no mention of them exploring the various bodily organs any further than stuffing them into a jar full of salt and shelving them. Exactly how the Egyptians first came about the idea of needing specific organs for this alleged afterlife – liver, intestines, lungs and stomach – is a mystery, especially when they left the heart in the body (being considered the "seat of the soul" as far as intelligence and feeling was concerned). This becomes more confusing when we consider the paradox of storing some organs in jars, "because they were needed in the afterlife," and leaving other organs in-situ for the exact same reason. But then, when it comes to the enigma of what happens to us after death, logic seems to fly out the window and we're left with our own ideas on the subject, however unprovable they are to us on the corporeal plane.

Okay, back to our elaborate blood ritual. The rest of the bull, being the flesh, hide and intestines, was to be taken outside the camp, it being referred to as a *"sin offering"* (Ex. 29:14). Not that it was a sin to offer it, of course, but rather it was to absolve the offeror of any sins he may have inadvertently committed in the course of his day. Personally, you would think that your "sin offering" would want to be done in the presence of your god as opposed to being conducted outside the camp, so that the big guy would know you're sorry for doing that kinky sex thing with the goat or whatever. I suppose they had their reasons, though. So now, they're ordered to take one of the rams and perform the hand-on-its-head thing while they slit its throat, and splash the blood on the sides of the altar (sounds more demonic with every verse!). This is followed by completely eviscerating and dismembering the animal and burning it in its entirety on the altar. We are told once more that this, *"is a burnt offering to the LORD, a pleasing aroma, a food offering presented to the LORD"* (Ex. 29:18). I get it, the dude likes his roast lamb. Or whatever man-sheep meat is called. Hogget, most probably, or perhaps mutton, although we generally call the meat "lamb" despite it being used for baby sheep; either way, it's certainly a better option than a date with Tom Cruise, even back in those days.

So we move onto the second ram now, which suffers a similar hands-on-its-head-and-slit-its-throat fate. The blood from this one, however, is used to adorn the right earlobes, right thumbs and right big toes of the priestly trio, and the rest gets splashed onto the altar again. Then the blood was scooped off the altar, combined with some of the anointing oil, and was "sprinkled" on Aaron and his priestly brats (Ex. 29:21). It makes me wonder why they made all that effort into washing them with water, only to tip oil and blood all over them afterward. It also makes me wonder if today's wandering bands of God Botherers even realize that these gruesome rituals are contained in their Good Book. I lean toward the negative.

After these grisly anointings, the liver lobe, kidneys, fat, tail fat, the fat from the organs, and the right thigh are liberated from the hapless animal, and along with some unyeasted bread is given to Aaron, for him to, *wave them before the LORD as a wave offering* (Ex. 29:24), before this too is burned on the altar for the whole Pleasing Aroma thing. Sounds very much like the sort of thing you'd do to get a cat to come eat its dinner; the only thing missing being the tapping on the side of the tin saying, "Heeere, Goddy Goddy Goddy, who's a good boy then..?!" Although by definition, once the wave offering was done, the item offered was then considered to belong to the priest offering it, which then seems like a bit of a tease, a bit like saying, "Nyer, nyer, look what I got..!" before eating the morsel at your target audience.

The next few verses concern themselves with how Aaron and his brats always get the breast and thigh of the offering, and the unyeasted bread in the basket, insisting that, *"no one else may eat them, because they are sacred"* (Ex. 29:33). This verse is nothing short of Aaron and Sons ensuring they get the best cuts of meat from any given animal; and by regular, ritual sacrifice to, "atone for perceived sins," also ensures that they'll never go hungry regardless of the availability of food to the masses. A self-serving act of greed that has only become worse over the millennia. Fast forward to today, and we see the untold wealth of the Catholic Church on display for all to see, oceans of gold and rare gems adorning every surface, yet there are still millions of people living in abject poverty. Even worse, we have "televangelists" who claim that God wants them to have another $54million Learjet, or live in million-dollar mansions while their ovine-like followers willingly hand over their 10% tithe to them despite being completely unable to afford such an outgoing, or pay over five thousand dollars to be in the same room as that charlatan. It's utterly disgusting, predatory and counter to the very moral principles Religion is supposed to represent and uphold, yet they consistently get away with it; and furthermore, pay no taxes on that money. This seriously needs to change, or we will never progress as a species.

Further evidence for this self-serving behaviour presents itself as we go along: *"This is what you are to offer on the altar regularly each day: two lambs a year old. Offer one in the morning and one at twilight"* (Ex. 29:38 – 29:39). How coincidental that this would be the times a person would normally be hungry; on waking up and after a day's work. Combined, of course, with some nice bread and a quarter of a hin of wine as a newly-invented Drink Offering. For clarity, a hin is equal to 1.5 gallons, or 5.7 litres; therefore one quarter of a hin would be about 1.425 litres of booze for the priests, twice a day. I'm in the wrong job..!

So it seems that Moses and Aaron and his brats have taken full advantage of this situation and set up themselves and their descendants pretty much indefinitely, so long as they keep to their story of being Chosen and sacred and burning the right things and wailing the right words, and as long as the Hebrew people don't wake up to their shenanigans. So far, nobody seems to have called them on their bluff, even today. Sad, really, that this entrenched indoctrination has such a profound hold on peoples' ability to engage their critical thinking and question the unquestionable. Let's move on.

Exodus 30: Speaking of Money..

"Religion has actually convinced people that there's an invisible man, living in the sky, who watches everything you do every minute of every day of your life. And he has a list of ten things he doesn't want you to do. And if you do any of these ten things, he has a special place full of fire and smoke and ash and torture where he will send you to suffer and burn and scream and cry for ever and ever until the end of time. But he loves you. He loves you, and he needs money!" -George Carlin

Another chapter of boring, OCD instructions for extravagant gold-encrusted fripperies, yay! Are we still convinced in our hearts that Moses was eidetic enough to remember the exacting dimensions and measurements of all these objects and tents and rules and laws and caveats and other demands from this crazy God, despite being well into his eighties? Or do we lean heavily on Occam's Razor and suppose that he made it all up as he went along, with just enough cunning to make sure he and his brother were set up for life, thanks to some obscure god-like entity? Let's see what we're told we have to do now so we don't die or get cut off or whatever punishment God has in store for non-compliance.

The Altar of Incense

First up, we're treated to God's instructions for yet another altar to be constructed, this time to be overlaid with gold and used for burning his favourite brand of incense. Like the other ones, this is also built with acacia wood and measuring one cubit square, and two cubits high, with all the requisite moldings and horns to adorn with sacrificial blood and so on. This one only needs the odd splash of blood once a year to atone for whatever sins have occurred that may have avoided atonement from the other, larger altars and sacrifices. This altar was to be lit day and night to make the joint smelly enough so God didn't have to deal with Human Stank™, and furthermore that no grain, burnt or drink offerings were done on it, nor was any other incense to be used on it apart from God's Favourite, a concoction of gum resin, Onycha, galbanum and frankincense reserved for the exclusive use of this finicky God. Whatever else you could say about all this exclusive-use bullshit, it at least drove the economy.

Atonement Money

People, even Moses and his peeps, cannot get along very far just with a permanent supply of grub, although it goes a very long way toward making life easier. With any sufficiently large group of people there develops an economy, be it by barter, trade exchange or currency, and we find here that Moses has accounted for this contingency as well, as we read here: *"When you take a census of the Israelites to count them, each one must pay the LORD a ransom for his life at the time he is counted. Then no plague will come on them when you number them"* (Ex. 30:12).

Why the hell would God, who allegedly created the universe with a snap of his fingers (well, except for that whole Adam's Rib thing), even *need* money? What possible thing would God want to buy with money that he couldn't either create himself, or demand from his followers? We've already seen how he's demanded the best meats and fruits and reserved his own bloody incense, among other things, so why the sudden grab for cash, on pain of additional plagues for non-compliance? More likely, Mose is using this wave of religious fervor to extort as much as he can from these gullible ex-slaves. And because we're painfully aware of the self-serving streak of malevolence running through Moses' bloodlines all the way back to Crazy Old Abe and beyond, it should really be no surprise to us that he would be taking full personal advantage of the situation, promising a plague-free life in exchange for material gain – for Moses, at least. In a way, it was history's first fear-based life insurance policy that would never be collected on.

Furthermore: *"Each one who crosses over to those already counted is to give half a shekel, according to the sanctuary shekel, which weighs twenty gerahs"* (Ex. 30:13). This was required of everyone over the age of twenty, and rich and poor alike had to pony up this half-shekel as ransom come census time. So it turns out that shekels were actually units of weight at this time, rather than currency, although this situation changed as society progressed. Still, a sanctuary shekel (or twenty gerahs) was a weight equal to 11.6 grams. So a half-shekel ransom would equate to 5.8 grams per person over the age of twenty. If we are to suppose that this would be the weight of silver – remember that Joseph was sold to Potiphar for twenty shekels of silver, and later on Judas sold out Jesus for thirty – and we also recall the bible's assertions of some 603,550 men over the age of twenty (to say nothing of the women), we're looking at a census collection of 3,500,590 grams (or just over *3.5 tonnes*) of silver. Even at today's modest price of fifty-one cents per gram, Moses would have completed the census with a $1.75 million fortune on his hands.

Shall we ask ourselves again why God would want all that silver? If we consider today's industrial uses for the metal, we find that silver is vital to the creation of many of today's modern tech, such as touch-screens, LED chips, photovoltaic energy production through solar panels, water purification and several medical applications, RFID chips, semiconductors, and is even used in nuclear reactors (along with other elements) to absorb neutrons without fissioning itself. If God was the technologically-advanced space-dude we're supposing here, it's possible that he used the silver to repair the ship's systems that were damaged and/or depleted on arrival at this unremarkable rock. Whether he actually used the whole 3.5 tonnes of it is up for debate, but you would think a fortune that large would have been mentioned at least once down the ages. Given the density of silver – volume-wise, each half-shekel would have occupied just over 0.5 cubic cm – the volume of 603,550 half-shekels would equate to about 0.3 cubic metres (the size of your average milk crate), assuming all that silver was melted into a solid block eliminating the empty space between the shekels. It was unlikely to be the case, however, considering the logistics needed; it's bad enough in today's world trying to break a $100 note at times, let alone a nomadic tribe trying to get the correct change for a 3.5 tonne block of silver. Let's just presume they chucked it all inna chest on the back of some wheeled contrivance and move on, shall we? Good.

The Basin of Washing

Next up, G-man wants a bronze basin, replete with bronze stand, out the front of his meeting tent, so that when Aaron and his brats go to enter the tent, they can wash their hands and feet with water, *"so that they will not die"* (Ex. 30:20), with the usual Lasting Ordinance spiel to make it sound official. This terminal threat is repeated for when Aaron and Co. are presenting a food offering to the G-man (also Ex. 30:20), because the last thing he wants is a dose of gastro, just because some goat-herding git didn't wash his mitts after wiping his arse. It's not a convincing look, trying to appear all omnipotent when you're face-down throwing your lungs up into a bucket, whilst simultaneously performing the unGodly Trots into another bucket from the other end of the gastric tract. It's not the kind of image to inspire awe, except from an olfactory perspective. Let's see what's next.

The Anointing Oil

What's next? Why, more absurd demands for material stuff, of course! God's next command for Moses is to secure, "500 shekels (about 5.7 litres) of liquid myrrh, 250 shekels of fragrant cinnamon, 250 of fragrant calamus, 500 of cassia and a hin (about 5.7 litres) of olive oil. Anyway, all of this crap was required to, *make these into a sacred anointing oil, a fragrant blend, the work of a perfumer*" (Ex. 30:25). Again, I am forced to ask where the ex-slave Hebrews would be finding these myriad artisans. Even if there were slaves working for a perfumery, their involvement in the process would be rudimentary at best (i.e. gathering and/or storing ingredients, cleaning utensils et al) rather than concocting perfumes themselves, the precise recipes known only to the master perfumer and shrouded in secrecy. No matter. I suppose in this instance, G-man has ordered his own Special Blend, and any idiot can follow a recipe if it's written down for him in small enough words. The other question is where they managed to secure such precious ingredients; myrrh, for instance, was once considered to be more precious than gold, so what were a bunch of ex-slaves doing with it? Yes, they extorted the Egyptians out of all their gold and silver when they rabbited, but a lot of that has been used in building all these bloody arks and tables and tabernacles and whatnot. It is amusing to consider that these Israelites were probably the richest community in the ancient world, if we consider the sheer volume of gold, silver and precious substances they're throwing about with gay abandon. For a people known for crying Persecution, they're doing pretty bloody well for themselves, it has to be said.

A further exhortation to proclaim this unique blend is for the use of G-man and his lackeys only, and that anyone else using it on anyone other than a priest, *"must be cut off from their people"* (Ex. 30:33). The practical meaning of this being, naturally, to be put to death, because Jealous God wouldn't let someone just wander off by themselves in a cloud of Jealous God's fragrance, now would he?

Incense

More work for the perfumer here, with an order for incense containing, *"gum resin, onycha, galbanum and pure frankincense, all in equal amounts"* (Ex. 30:34), which was to be salted, pure and sacred. Additionally, some of it was to be ground into a powder and put in front of the covenant ark, with the usual threat of death for anyone using it other than God and his priests. And that's it for that chapter.

Exodus 31: God distributes Skill Points (SKP)

"What your interests are has a lot to do with your natural abilities." -Lee Haney.

In our last few chapters, we've had to fight our way through some astonishingly detailed dimensions and measurements and volumes of myriad crap that no octogenarian anywhere could possibly remember with any accuracy. Just for fun, run all these figures to someone at a nursing home and tell them there'll be a test on it later that day; I'll be interested to see the results. Anyway, it's been quite boring and distracting from our narrative, but necessary if only to cover all the bases. And despite this part of Exodus attempting to divert our attention from that dodgy narrative, we've still found a few logistical anomalies that run counter to the mental image of a poor, persecuted people. In fact, it only highlighted the idea that Moses was manipulating everyone in a big scam designed to install him and his family into a position of extreme material wealth and luxury, provided they keep up a pretense of wailing odd things and adhering to strange rituals. Now, whether that was as a result of capitalizing on a real-life event or merely the product of his own twisted imagination, only Moses knew. Regardless of the cause, it has certainly stood the test of time and been carried on in our imaginations for generations. Moses is probably pissing himself laughing at our prolonged gullibility.

Aaanyway, let's crack on with it. We kick off with God rapping to Moses again – no mention of where that happened or who else was involved in that conversation, mind you – and saying, *"See, I have chosen Bezalel son of Uri, son of Hur, of the tribe of Judah, and filled him with the Spirit of God, with wisdom, with understanding, with knowledge and with all kinds of skills"* (Ex. 31:1 – 31:2). How generous of this mysterious God to hand out skills and abilities like door prizes, as if they hadn't occurred naturally as part of natural human curiosity. One day, Bezalel is a drooling dipshit; the next he's a Renaissance Man able to create designs for (and also create) metalworks precious and mundane, cut and set stone, perform woodwork and myriad other crafts as required by the G-man. Judging by previous assertations, I'm going to run with the assertion that God is taking credit for shit he didn't do again. It's not the first time, and it certainly won't be the last. Anyway, God then mentions that he's *"appointed Oholiab son of Ahisamak to help"* (Ex. 31:6), saying further that he has, *"given ability to all the skilled workers to make everything I have commanded you"* (also Ex. 31:6). Well, that's nice, that means Moses isn't making all this crap by himself as was the inference in previous chapters, but the method of conferring that knowledge intrigues me. Did

God simply stream the knowledge and ability into their heads like you would fill up a hard drive with bootleg movies? Did he wire their skulls with USB ports and plug in a flash drive or two? Did he disseminate instruction manuals? Were there special night classes involved (guaranteed no idle chatter in *that* classroom!)? More than likely, Moses just found these people in the course of his musings and convinced them that his God gave them their myriad abilities in order to serve him, and he took advantage of those skills for zero labour costs (because it was a Divine Work, of course) with materials sourced in exactly the same way, i.e. through fraudulent deception. We could almost dismiss such cunning artifice in ancient man, were it not for the records of his ancestors (Jacob/Israel/whatever, Isaac, Crazy Old Abe, etc.), so that behaviour is definitely coded into that inbred blood of theirs.

More Sabbath Nonsense

As if we haven't heard it enough already, God then reiterates that the Sabbath is to be strictly observed through the generations, *"so that you may know that I am the Lord, who makes you holy"* (Ex. 31:13). I'm a bit confused by this one. How does lounging around doing nothing one day in every seven allow you to "know" that God exists? Yes, this is supposed to be a tribute to God's whole "created-the-universe-in-six-days-

and-rested-on-the-seventh" thing covered in Genesis, but what is this imitation achieving? Is it supposed to be some sort of enforced introspection about who's boss around here? Why can't that soul searching be conducted on a regular day, whilst going about your work? There are certainly enough hours in the day to allow some of them to be employed in quiet contemplation, keeping the rabble honest and fearful and all that jazz. With so many rules that require death as punishment for non-compliance, I would imagine the need for proper conduct would be at the forefront of everyone's mind, without the need for a whole day to dwell upon it.

To wit: *"Observe the Sabbath, because it is holy to you. Anyone who desecrates it is to be put to death; those who do any work on that day must be cut off from their people"* (Ex. 31:14). Additionally: *"Whoever does any work on the Sabbath day is to be put to death"* (Ex. 31:15). So, the previous interpretation I made of the phrase "cut off from their people" as meaning, "put to death" back in Ex. 30:33 (the incense bit) seems to be emphatically borne out by these two verses. It certainly lends weight to the claim that this God of the Israelites is violently, murderously intolerant of even the slightest infraction. Given that to be the case, would you *really* need a whole fricking day every week doing nothing except comprehending what a petty, insecure deity you're stuck worshipping? Given a choice in the matter, I reckon most of them would happily push this vengeful, bloodthirsty god under the ethereal bus and pray for a Thoth or an Osiris or even a Horus. There were about two thousand of them all up at one stage, so there were plenty of options to score a nice minor god with aspirations toward greatness. Perhaps Aker, God of Earth (sand) got jiggy with Jedjhotep, bi-sexual goddess of clothing, and made Adjherhot, who wandered the earth putting sand in the underpants of the impious, and missed out on being worshipped by the Hebrews only by chance. I dare anyone to prove me wrong, but if the God of the Hebrews did have sand in his undies because Adjherhot was getting his own back, it would explain a great many of God's behaviours.

Finally, we are told, *"When the LORD finished speaking to Moses on Mount Sinai, he gave him the two tablets of the covenant law, the tablets of stone inscribed by the finger of God"* (Ex. 31:18). Good grief, might we possibly raise our hopes of the bible returning to its narrative? It sounds like it, so let's cross our fingers and see what transpires in our next chapter. No mention of Moses also carrying parchments of weights, measures and dimensions for all these arks and tables and tabernacles and such to relay to the parties charged with building all this stuff for him, though. But hey, he's well into his eighties by now; how bad a memory can he have..?

Inscribing the stone tablets
with the Finger of God...

Exodus 32: When The Cat's Away...

"Genocide is not just a murderous madness; it is, more deeply, a politics that promises a utopia beyond politics – one people, one land, one truth, the end of difference. Since genocide is a form of political utopia, it remains an enduring temptation in any multiethnic and multicultural society in crisis." - Michael Ignatieff.

Meanwhile, back at the ranch, the refugeebews were getting restless waiting for Moses to come back from his mountain pow-wow with God. We find them gathering around Aaron and saying, *"Come, make us gods who will go before us. As for his fellow Moses who brought us out of Egypt, we don't know what has happened to him"* (Ex. 32:1). I suppose you can't really blame the buggers, milling about the bottom of Sinai for a month with no apparent activity beyond a weird cloud bank obscuring most of the mountain and an "await further instruction" order from a crazy 80+ year old man. And after a week of no smiting, even the simplest of them could be forgiven for trying to find their own direction. Anyway, Aaron takes their request on board, commands them to bring him the gold earrings adorning their family members and made, *"an idol cast into the shape of a calf, fashioning it with a tool"* (Ex. 32:2 – 32:4). Then, *"they said, 'These are your gods, Israel, who brought them out of Egypt.'"* Now, it's unclear if "they" (I presume the refugeebrews) had intended this golden calf to be a physical representation of God, or whether the use of the plural and small "g" in "gods" meant that they intended it to be their new soothsaying tool for use in divination as they were accustomed to in Genesis (think back to Rachel's stealing of her father's "gods" and hiding them under her camel's saddle, and then claiming her period to avoid their discovery back in Gen. 31:35). We'll read further: *"When Aaron saw this, he built an altar in front of the calf and announced, 'Tomorrow there will be a festival to the LORD"* (Ex. 31:5).

When Aaron saw what, exactly? That the peeps called the calf their gods? That he saw what he had made? That the people were cool with their new idol? It could be interpreted pretty much any way that suits you, to be honest. Whatever the reason, we have it sitting behind an altar now, for peeps to worship or soothsay or wail or whatever they did back then. And on the morrow, they did their sacrifices and worships and offerings, then laid back to eat, drink and indulge in a little light revelry, as one tends to do (Ex. 31:6).

Unfortunately for the refugeebrews, they were being observed. Next thing, God is telling Moses to hotfoot it down the mountain to his peeps because his people, *"have become corrupt"* (Ex. 32:7), telling Mose all about the gold calf and the sacrifices and revelry and so forth.

Then God says, *"Leave me alone so that my anger may burn against them and that I may destroy them. Then I will make you into a great nation"* (Ex. 32:10). Hmm, that's going to be pretty hard to do, G; destroy the lot of them, and then make them into a great nation. There won't be any "them" left to make a great nation, unless you're going to dip into the Clay-Doh™ barrel again and roll out some more whiney Israelites for Mose to lord it over. Silly immortal twat…

Moses, for his part, pleads for the defense, stating, *"Why should the Egyptians say, 'It was with evil intent that he brought them out, to kill them in the mountains and wipe them off the face of the earth?'"* (Ex. 32:12). Then Mose chucks God's promises of land and prosperity he made to Abe and Isaac and Israel/Jacob back in his face, to seal the deal. Pretty gutsy move to make on a vengeful smitey god, Mose; you got some stones on you, bro..!

Now, any vengeful god worth his salt pillar would have smited – smote - the bloody lot of them right there and then and found himself another tribe to terrorize. But amazingly, God turns the other cheek and reneges on his vow to kill 'em all. I know we haven't got to the Jesus stuff yet, but we can amuse ourselves by thinking he was in there yelling to himself not to go about killing shit all the time; an internal

Freudian battle between the Id, the Ego and the SuperEgo on the immortal scale, if you will.

So Moses hoofs it down the mountain lugging the two stone commandment tablets, which is really stupid because he still had Joshua with him, who was at least half his age and more easily able to carry the tablets than a man who's pushing ninety; but whatever. As they near the camp, they can hear shouting and Joshua thinks it's the sound of war in the camp. Moses has the right of it (being told, of course, by God) and says that it's not the sound of victory or defeat, but singing that can be heard (Ex. 32:18).

Now it gets interesting: *"When Moses approached the camp and saw the calf and the dancing, his anger burned and he threw the tablets out of his hands, breaking them to pieces at the foot of the mountain"* (Ex. 32:19). No angry beratement of the people prior to the tablet chucking, as Hollywood would have us believe, and no thundery accompaniment. Just a "WTF" moment and a dummy spit. This is especially silly when we're told that God himself chiseled (well, fingered) the commands onto those tablets, only to have Mose smash them before anyone could see him do it, apart from Joshua. That action in and of itself would have been enough for an unstable God to smite his arse and find a new leader. Oh well.

Now we discover the extent of Moses' anger: *"And he took the calf the people had made and burned it in the fire; then he ground it to powder, scattered it on the water and made the Israelites drink it"* (Ex. 32:20). He must've been royally pissed to have been able to burn gold (which requires 1,064°C just to melt it, about 400°C higher than your average campfire) and then grind it to a powder (which would have taken forever using ancient techniques), let alone making an aqueous solution with the stuff and force-feeding ... force-*watering* ... over 600,000 Israelites. That's a righteously-sustained anger burn right there.

After Moses' fit of pique, he barreled Aaron up and asked, *"What did these people do to you, that you led them into such great sin?"* (Ex. 32:21). Aaron pleads innocence, claiming, *"You know how prone these people are to evil"* (Ex. 32:22), describing how he was approached by them to make gods for them to follow, so he asked them for their gold jewellery.

Then this: *"Then they gave me the gold, and I threw it into the fire, and out came this calf!"* (Ex. 32:24). Wow. Talk about your all-time, the-dog-ate-my-homework, blame-directing bullshit! But you can't blame Aaron for trying it on and claiming a calf figure via divine formation, despite the idol undoubtedly bearing evidence of physical forming from Aaron's "tool" when he fashioned the thing. Having met God briefly on the mountain, he was most likely shitting bricks at this stage and keeping a wary eye on the horizon for approaching thunderclouds. Meanwhile, Moses was watching the Israelites running amok under Aaron's watch and, *"so become a laughingstock to their enemies"* (Ex. 32:25), which impressed ol' Mose not one little bit.

He summarily stood at the edge of the camp and commanded, *"Whoever is for the LORD, come to me,"* at which the Levites instantly complied, the Levites being Aaron's clan, of course (Ex. 32:26). Followed by, *"This is what the LORD, God of Israel, says: 'Each man strap a sword to his side. Go back and forth through the camp from one end to the other, each killing his brother and friend and neighbour"* (Ex. 32:27), in an ancient parody of Order 66; and the Levites happily set to with their swords, slaughtering about three thousand people (Ex. 32:38).

Well okay, I hear you say, three thousand people out of over six hundred thousand is barely half of one percent of the population; no big deal, right? It's hardly a genocide by any means, and it would barely make a blip in the numbers you'd get for natural attrition through age and infirmity versus birth replenishment. But something still didn't sit right with these numbers, so I had a look ahead to Numbers to see how many Levites there were in the Sinai Census; it turns out that between the Gershon, Kohath and Merari clans, there were approximately 22,300 males aged over one month old. So if we reasonably consider, say, a third to a half of this number were either too young or too old to wield a sword (based on today's population age distribution trends), this still leaves between eleven and fifteen thousand males running through the camp with bloody intent, meaning that each armed Levite killed approximately 20-25% of a person. Or put another way, it took about four or five Levites armed with swords to take down one sinful reveler. And you think today's law enforcement has issues with methamphetamine! Either that, or there was a large percentage of the male Levite population that wasn't pulling its weight that day.

Once this bout of random slaughter was done, Moses then opined, *"You have been set apart to the LORD today, for you were against your own sons and brothers, and he has blessed you this day"* (Ex. 32:29). Just another prime example of the requirements for membership to the Abrahamic religion, really: Be a thieving, conniving, blame-deflecting, murderous, traitorous sack of shit who does exactly what he/she is told without question, and God will love you. These Levites have unquestioningly run through a camp of humans slaughtering thousands of otherwise-innocent people, and because of that they are supposed to be favoured by God? I suppose it makes a kind of perverse sense when we place God into the "murderously insane" category of deities, but then who in their right mind would willingly worship such a creature? Modern day Christians rabbit on about Satan-worshippers performing dubious rituals that are generally considered "evil," but these same Christians should, perhaps, actually read what's in their own book and realize how many parallels there are to the Satanism they despise. Perhaps the only difference between religiously "good" and "evil" is the choice of worship? If we skip up to Leviticus 16, we find the use of "scapegoats" to cleanse the priests of sin, etc., and therefore associating goats with evil, while they happily slaughter lambs for blessings. What if the only original difference between that and Satanism was the esteem afforded to goats compared to lambs? Religious cults over the millennia have slaughtered each other for far less.

Back to the narrative, though: after this bloody and needless slaughter, Moses then addresses the people and tells them they've all been really bad and sinful, but that he'll hoof it back up the mountain to God and, *"perhaps I can make atonement for your sin"* (Ex. 32:30). The old, "keep 'em scared, keep 'em hanging" method of crowd control. So Mose goes clambering up the mountainside again and raps with G-man, wailing about how sinful his people have been and imploring God to forgive their sins, *"but if not, then blot me out of the book you have written"* (Ex. 32:32). So it was actually God himself who wrote the bible, was it? I believe we touched on that issue when I covered the Applegate saga in Genesis 3 (The Fall, and why talking animals should not be trusted). I can't really see God recording his memoirs with any accuracy when Genesis had more holes in its narrative than a proverbial swiss cheese. It's more likely that Moses was the original author of these texts, if only to install himself and his family line above everyone else, and this verse was simply to add weight to this deception. But because religion will have you believe it all actually happened, we will have fun poking even more holes in the assertion (which is why you're all still here reading this, obviously!).

The reply from God is equally predictable: *"Whoever has sinned against me I will blot out of my book.* (aww, boo-hoo.) *Now go lead the people to the place I spoke of, and my angel will go before you. However, when the time comes for me to punish, I will punish them for their sin"* (Ex. 32:33 – 32:34). Then we have our final verse for the chapter, *"And the LORD struck the people with a plague because of what they did with the calf Aaron had made."* (Ex. 32:35). So really, God doesn't care who he smites with plagues or death or whatever, so long as *someone* is suffering and he's getting his regular meals of roast lamb on golden plates and mugs and tables, and smelly incense to mask the aroma of shit coming from the clueless rabble milling around outside his tent thinking he's All That. Or are we actually talking about Moses here instead of God, if we are to think about it on a more prosaic level? My money is on the latter.

Exodus 33: To See or Not To See

"Oceanic society rests ultimately on the belief that Big Brother is omnipotent and that the Party is infallible. But since in reality Big Brother is not omnipotent and the party is not infallible, there is need for an unwearying moment-to-moment flexibility in the treatment of facts. The keyword here is BLACKWHITE. Like so many Newspeak words, this word has two mutually contradictory meanings. Applied to an opponent, it means the habit of impudently claiming that black is white, in contradiction of the plain facts. Applied to a Party member, it means a loyal willingness to say that black is white when Party discipline demands this. But it means also the ability to BELIEVE that black is white, and more, to KNOW that black is white, and to forget that one has ever believed the contrary." -George Orwell, 1984.

As you may have suspected from the larger-than-usual quote above, anyone who has read and enjoyed George Orwell's "1984" and finds fault with the bible will enjoy this chapter. We already have plenty of ammunition under our belts with the previous thirty two chapters and the entirety of Genesis, but there is no such thing as, "Too Much Ammunition" when you get right down to it.

And so we begin. The first six verses largely concern themselves with God talking to Moses and telling him to hoof it off to, *"the land I promised on oath to Abraham Isaac and Jacob, saying, 'I will give it to your descendants"* (Ex. 33:1). So far so good, we still have an as-yet unfulfilled promise without a delivery date and no perceived statute of limitations. Situation Normal, as they say. Another promise of sending an angel before them to drive out those pesky Canaanites, Jebusites, Hittites, Hivites and so on so that the refugeebrews can walk on in to this *"land flowing with milk and honey. But I will not go with you, because you are a stiff-necked people and I might destroy you on the way"* (Ex. 33:3). I've personally never seen a river of milk, nor honey, although I've seen some pretty dodgy water coming out of drinking taps that looked like it'd been filtered through limestone and had all the appearance of milk. Perhaps there is a river in the promised land that has this opaque quality. And we're still on-track in regards to God proclaiming to love his chosen peeps but wanting to kill them all at the same time. I guess that's no different to the feelings inside the breast of every parent on the planet, ever, in regards to their own offspring and their youthful foibles.

Now comes the first of our BLACKWHITE references. First up, *"When the people heard these distressing words, they began to mourn and no one put on any ornaments"* (Ex. 33:4). Followed immediately by this: *"For the LORD said to Moses, 'Tell the Israelites, "You are a stiff-necked*

256

people. If I were to go with you even for a moment, I might destroy you. Now take off your ornaments and I will decide what to do with you."'" (Ex. 33:5).

So which is it? Did the people hear the actual words from God's mouth and decide not to wear ornaments out of mourning off their own bat, as Ex. 33:4 suggests? Or did Moses just command the people to take off their ornaments as some sort of disciplinary penance as claimed by Ex. 33:5? It was either one or the other, Moses; the two verses are mutually exclusive, so pick a struggle, dude!

Regardless of which verse it was, the Israelites summarily stripped off their ornaments at Mount Horeb (Ex. 33:6) and no correspondence was entered into. Knowing Moses the way we do now, it wouldn't surprise me in the slightest if he just made up that little tidbit in order to get the Israelites to remove their jewelry, so he could pick it up for himself later. I wouldn't put it past him, to be honest.

The Tent of Meeting

Here we are told that Moses was in the habit of pitching a tent outside the main camp, *"some distance away"* and call it the Tent of Meeting, where anyone who wanted to rap with God could rock up and Moses would do his voodoo shit to get the big guy to come down and make whatever judgments were deemed necessary. The narrative goes on to say that, *"whenever*

Moses went out to the tent, all the people rose and stood at the entrances to their tents, watching Moses until he entered the tent" (Ex. 33:8). This behaviour would continue when Moses entered the tent and a *"pillar of cloud"* would descend to the entrance to this Meeting Tent, ostensibly God talking to Moses. Whatever. It was more likely that the pillar of cloud was merely smoke from the incense billowing out of the tent and rising instead of descending. Think, *"Cheech and Chong's Up In Smoke"* for a suitable mental image of the tent.

Now here's the really important verse to remember here, because we'll come back to it again very soon: *"The LORD would speak to Moses face to face, as one speaks to a friend"* (Ex. 33:11). Then Moses would wander back to his own tent, but apparently Joshua son of Nun would not leave this tent. Nobody knows why.

Moses and the Glory of the LORD

This part is interesting to me, for the sheer departure from Reality you need to undertake to reconcile it with everything else we're being told here. We start with Moses asking God who will go with him to this promised land; that he should lead these people, but hasn't been told much else in regard to the details. I find that hard to believe when he's been given detailed instructions on just about every other bloody thing in regards to worshipping this diva God.

How can God give this guy complex lists and dimensions of objects to be made with exacting measurements and materials, and yet be utterly vague about where they're going or who is going to accompany them on their odyssey? It doesn't add up; I reckon Moses is just making it up as he goes along, and had a bit of a brain fart (or a mini-stroke) concerning their destination. Whatever. God's all like, *"My Presence will go with you,"* and Moses is like, *"If it doesn't, then don't send us up from here,"* claiming that nobody will know they're the Chosen Peeps if he's not there to verify the claims (a fair point) and asking what else distinguishes him from the rest of the earth's rabble.

God then says that he *"will do the very thing you have asked, because I am pleased with you and I know you by name"* (Ex. 33:17). What an odd thing for a God to say. We are constantly told that God is omniscient, so why wouldn't he know *everyone* by name? Isn't that the whole crux of the Christian argument? God sees every thing you do, knows all your thoughts, so you better bloody well toe the line, old son. It makes the claim of having a "personal relationship with God" laughable at best, if God only does things if he knows who you are, which he should do anyway if he's supposed to know everything. Again, pick a struggle.

So Moses gathers his stones and says, *"Show me your glory"* (Ex. 33:18). And God is all like, *"I will cause all my goodness to pass in front of you,"* and blah blah blah, not important, read it for yourself later if you wish. This bit here, though, is the kicker: *"But,"* he said, *"you cannot see my face, for no one may see me and live"* (Ex. 33:20).

Three words, readers: What. Da. Fuq.

Unless you're an expert in BLACKWHITE or you're completely Out To Lunch, there is no possible way to hold Ex. 33:11 and 33:20 in your mind and accept them both as truth:

- 33:11 – The LORD would speak to Moses face to face, as one speaks to a friend;

- 33:20 – But you cannot see my face, for no one may see me and live.

I would be greatly interested in reader feedback should you get accosted by a door-knocking God Botherer to clarify this point of order - correspondence to the usual addresses – but for me, there is only one logical reason for this:

"God" is no longer "God."

He may have touted himself as all-seeing, all-knowing and all-wise, but he was also just a physical being. Was he much older? Was he sick? Was he replaced or usurped by the crew of his ship? Had he suffered a serious accident? Had he, in fact, died? Not a good look if you've spent your life letting a bunch of goat herders think you're immortal, is it? So, it's entirely possible that the crew of Yahweh's ship, having removed him from command or finding him dead on the toilet seat from a meal of bad lamb roast, find themselves without their figurehead to the Israelites. And so, like anyone would do in that position, they found a crew member most resembling Yahweh, kitted him up in his customary clothing, and kept the illusion going, with the caveat that, *"my face must not be seen"* because even a goat-herder would recognize that it was not the same guy he was talking to a week earlier across the dinner table.

Anyway, this "God 2.0" mentions a rock nearby that Moses can stand on, with a convenient cleft in the rock that God himself will put Moses in, and, *"cover you with my hand until I have passed by. Then I will remove my hand and you will see my back; but my face must not be seen"* (Ex. 33:23).

So, as far as I'm interpreting this, God tells Moses to stand on this rock, then God's going to stuff him into the cleft in this rock and cover it with his hand while God passes by, and then removes his hand when he's got his back to Moses. If you have another interpretation, I'd like to hear it, but let's look at the logistics of this scenario:

Firstly, God gets Moses to stand on this rock. This would have elevated Moses' line of sight and he would have seen God approaching from any direction. And he wouldn't be concerned with not looking at God, because he's used to talking with him "face to face" anyway as 33:11 previously asserts.

Secondly, we have God sticking Moses in this cleft in the rock, and covering it with his hand. Now I'm about thirty inches (77cm) from shoulder to shoulder, so I can tell you now that I wouldn't want to be shoved into a cleft any narrower than that without a severe attack of claustrophobia; so the diameter of the cleft could not have been any less than this, and therefore God's hand could not have been any smaller than, say, eighty centimetres to cover this cleft sufficiently to hide his ugly mug from Moses. Given that length of hand, we can extrapolate at least from a human perspective (remember, we were apparently made in God's image) and determine that God stood just over seven metres tall. This is determined from a study that concluded that an individual's height is approximately nine times the length of their hand, give or take a smidge. If we take this to be true, it would also be in keeping with how the Nephilim came into being, when the "Sons of God" got jiggy with the "Daughters of Men" back in Genesis, creating this race of giants. If God and his peeps averaged heights of seven metres, that genetic trait would undoubtedly be passed on to any progeny. Good luck giving birth to *that* baby without ripping the poor woman from stem to stern, let alone getting a proportionally-sized phallus in there in the first place! Sadly, there are no reliable correlations between penis size and the overall height of a person, so we can only speculate wildly on what a seven-metre-tall humanoid might have between his legs. If we simply *must* hypothesize on the matter, then if we can agree that the average guy can have himself firmly "in-hand" as it were (barring conditions like micro-penis, a condition I strongly suspect God suffered given his mentality), we would have to allow that we're looking at a phallus between 70cm and 80cm in length, with a similar circumference which we divide by Pi, giving us a diameter of approximately 23.5cm. To put that into perspective, it would be similar to a human female being sexually violated by Arnold Schwarzenegger's upper leg at the height of his bodybuilding career. I don't care how many miles you've got on your vay-jay, ladies, there's *no* scenario where that's going to end well!

Thirdly, keeping the cleft in the rock covered until God had passed by would have presented some obvious biomechanical difficulties unless God was double-jointed, or at least kept his face averted as he adjusted the position of his hand during his procession past the rock cleft. But given he was supposedly rapping with Moses face to face as previously mentioned, the whole thing stinks of lies and fallacy.

Well, that chapter was both fun and disturbing, for the obvious respective reasons. We'll take a deep breath, let those of you who got all excited about Arnie's leg dimensions pop off to the bedroom for a while to get your head straight, before we plunge on to the next chapter. We understand, we can wait...!

Exodus 34: God's Increasing Insanity

"Roses are red, violets are blue, I'm schizophrenic, and so am I." -Oscar Levant

Okay, loyal readers, let's get ready for some more next-level Crazy™ to make even Orwell's head drown in Doublethink. We start this chapter with God telling Moses to chip out two more stone tablets to replace the ones he broke in his hissy fit, so that God can scribble all his commandments down on them again. Moses is told to be ready in the morning, and to present himself to G-man at the top of Mount Sinai. He is told in no uncertain terms, *"No one is to come with you or be seen anywhere on the mountain; not even the flocks and herds may graze in front of the mountain"* (Ex. 34:3). Well, good luck with that. If Mosey can't even keep his own people from toeing the line, how is he going to tell a flock of sheep to sod off? Who cares, that's his problem, not mine. It's a bit harsh, though, making him lug another two stone tablets up the mountain by his Pat Malone. It makes for a good story of personal hardship and sacrifice, however, so we'll run with it for now. He gets to the top of the mountain, and when he does, we have the whole cloud-coming-down-from-the-sky thing and God, *"stood there with him and proclaimed his name, the LORD"* (Ex. 34:5); despite us clearly being told in Ex. 3:14 that God's name was, "I AM" (or, as I reckon, "Ian"). I guess it depends on what particular personality is pushing itself to the front of his consciousness at the time, I've pretty much lost count of them at this point.

The following verse salvo pretty much proves this hypothesis: *"And he passed in front of Moses* (what, no hiding his face?), *proclaiming, 'The LORD, the LORD, the compassionate and gracious God, slow to anger, abounding in love and faithfulness, maintaining love to thousands, and forgiving wickedness, rebellion and sin. Yet he does not leave the guilty unpunished; he punishes the children and their children for the sin of the parents to the third and fourth generation"* (Ex. 34:6 – 34:7).

"Compassionate"..?! "Slow to anger"?!! Are you freaking *kidding* me?! "Forgiving wickedness and sin" and then in the very next breath, he's all about punishing innocent descendants for the next four generations! Please tell me the mindset required to hold these proclamations in your head all at once without your brain turning to toothpaste and oozing out your ears. You would have to push an icepick through your skull to drop your IQ to the level needed to believe this tripe! He claims being, *"slow to anger,"* and yet he can't travel with his own chosen people, *"even for one moment, I might destroy you,"* as previously claimed in Ex. 33:5. He claims to be "compassionate," and yet, the plagues, even on his own chosen peeps. Does this guy even listen to what he's saying, or is it just psychotic babble? To put it bluntly, God's arse must be jealous of the shit coming out of his mouth. God might believe this shit, but any rational-thinking human would have too many pointed questions to believe a single word of it.

Moses, of course, drops to the ground and does some grovelly worshipping, asking for God's favour and to forgive his "stiff-necked people" and to take them all as God's inheritance (Ex. 34:9). Personally, I would have preferred a nice tropical island to inherit instead of this pack of daft goat herders, but we have to play the hand that's dealt to us, yeah? Anyway, God replies to Moses and establishes a covenant with him, promising to, *"do wonders never before done in any nation in all the world,"* (Ex. 34:10) and big-noting how all the peeps will know just how awesome these wonders will be and blah blah blah (insert suggestive hand gesture here).

God then merely repeats the promise he made back in Genesis of driving all the Hittites and Canaanites and et cetera off their land (so compassionate is he), and telling them not to make any treaties with those displaced people because *"they will be a snare among them"* (letting that paranoia out for some fresh air, Ex. 34:12). Then he implores them to *"break down [these displaced peoples'] altars, smash their sacred stones and cut down their Asherah poles"* (Ex. 34:13) demonstrating his love of thousands. Then there's, *"Do not worship any other god, for the LORD, whose name is Jealous, is a jealous God"* (Ex. 34:14).

So, your name is Jealous now? Not "I AM" or "The LORD" or "Ian" or "Yahweh"? Whatever, you crazy bastard, we'll just add it to the rest of your ever-increasing list of personalities trying to get their voice heard above the general noise of insanity between your ears. At any rate, it makes a mockery of the whole, "compassionate and gracious god" claim. God goes on further about not treating with foreigners who "prostitute" themselves to their gods, for fear that his chosen peeps will follow suit, and the same for marrying outside their inbred little clique and being tempted into the worship of other gods. Which, as has been said on many occasions, cannot be the case if there was only one god who created the universe, unless we count the myriad personalities running amok in God's increasingly-psychotic bonce. The rest of the paragraph concerns itself with repeating pretty much everything God mentioned before in Exodus 23 in regards to yeast, and no boiling goats in their mother's milk, and the breaking of donkey necks and other such inanities. Meh. And we're told Mose spends another forty days and nights on the mountain without food or water writing all this shit down again. Either that or God was a bloody slow chiseler.

The Radiant Face of Moses

Finally, we read that Mose comes back down the mountainside, two fresh shiny stone tablets with God's commandments scratched into them, and we're led to believe that Moses' face was *"radiant because he had spoken to the LORD"* (Ex. 34:29). If you ask me, it was more likely that Moses was exposed to residual radiation from God's engines and can now be used as a human night light. The rest of the Israelites saw this glowy weirdness and were rightly fearful of getting too near the luminescent loony; but Moses called to them, apparently, and that was sufficient for them to crowd around and hear what Moses and God rapped about on the top of Sinai.

After he'd done that, Moses started covering his mug with a veil unless he was having a gasbag with the Big Guy, or when he was dictating the latest rule updates to the masses. And, in the words of Forrest Gump, "that's all we have to say about that."

Exodus 35 – 40: The Rape of the Israelites

"How do you milk sheep? With a collection plate."
-Me.

Yes, my dear readers, we're making a headlong dash to the finish line here, not for a lack of enthusiasm, but rather a lack of fresh content. For reasons known only to the original authors of the bible, they have seen fit to repeat what they put down back in Exoduses 25 to 29, pretty much verbatim except for a couple of extra bits and pieces which I shall winnow from the chaff of duplicated verses, which we can all agree can be utterly ignored. I mean, do you really want me to repeat all that boring crap about the ark and tabernacle dimensions and lampstands and washing bowls and priest garments and wave and sin offerings and bronze altars and so on? Well, *do you*?? Yeah, I didn't think so: one time around that literary block is quite enough and, given its tedious nature, is probably one time too many at that. If you're interested in that sort of thing, feel free to wander off and explore the full verses on your own; but as I say, they are covering what's already been said, and as such are redundant for the purposes of this book. If anything, it could be interpreted as an attempt to brainwash people by repetition, thinking that repeating something often enough will create credibility where none exists. Well, good luck with that, bible..!

Anyhoo, the basic premise of these chapters is that Moses called out to the Israelites and called for those who "were willing" to bring forth the offerings of gold, silver, bronze, and the rest of the rubbish he needed to make all the crap God needed to play Diva; also, for those willing to donate their time and skills to create the rods and poles and curtains and such. And here we were thinking God told Moses to make these things, not merely subcontract it to outsiders! I suppose when you look at the sheer number of outrageous requests, and Moses' advanced age, he could be forgiven this one expedient; but I still think it's cheating.

As far as skills go, Moses calls up his homie Bezalel and tells the peeps, *"See, the LORD has chosen Bezalel son of Uri … and filled him with the Spirit of God, with wisdom, with understanding, with knowledge and all kinds of mad skillz* (okay, creative license there) – *to make artistic designs in precious metals, to cut and set stones, to work in wood and engage in all kinds of artistic crafts. And he has given him and Ololiab son of Ahisamak the ability to teach others"* (Ex. 35:30 – 35:34), and other such rot. In truth, these two buggers were probably Da Vinci's ancestors and history's first Renaissance men, jacks of all trades and general smartarses who would probably get beaten up without divine protection.

Anyway, these two apparently made All The Things God had commanded Moses to build, with the possible exception of the incense which was, *"the work of a perfumer"* and thusfar remains an unnamed entity. As far as materials concerned, the (alleged) combined value of the metals used is recorded as:

Gold: 29 talents and 730 shekels;

Silver: 100 talents and 1,775 shekels;

Bronze: 70 talents and 2,400 shekels.

So what is this "talent" all of a sudden, I hear you ask, and why don't the shekels add up in a logical manner? Well, we know of the shekels of course, which is defined only as a "sanctuary shekel," a weight of 11.5 grams, and while it's typically associated with silver due to the "shekel" coin minted in later years, it seems the weight is the important thing, rather than the value of the metal itself. The talent, on the other hand, is regarded as a 33kg block of whatever metal you've got, which was divided into 60 minas, which were themselves divided into 60 skekels; therefore, one talent was roughly equal to 3,600 shekels. So, according to the above numbers, we can determine that this bloody big tent God wanted required (with its myriad accessories) approximately:

965.395 kilograms of gold;

3,320.4 kilograms of silver (or 3.3 tonnes as previously calculated); and

2,337.6 kilograms – 2.3 tonnes – of bronze.

Now, if we take this across the alleged 603,550 males over the age of twenty, this would mean that every single male would've had to pony up 1.6 grams of gold, 5.5 grams of silver and 3.87 grams of bronze. Not altogether unreasonable, assuming that every single person paid up and they still have all the gold and silver and crap they "liberated" (read: stole) from the hapless Egyptians prior to their escarpment. If we also assume the numbers were lower due to the slaughter of those 3,000 revelers and boost their "donation" due to their corpses being stripped of precious metals, the sizes are still feasible. And for the "greater glory" of God, a gold ring or a nub of silver isn't that much, especially if it wasn't yours to begin with. This goes to show just how insidious America's "mega-churches" are, pulling in tens of thousands of gullible people, some paying upwards of $6,000 for "prime seats" nearest the stage, and no doubt requiring a commensurate "plate donation" which are not even plates so much as they are plastic buckets to hold the sheer volume of the money they're collecting, "for God." And it's all *tax-free*.

Just let that sink in for a minute.

Does God get that money? Why should he even want it, when he can create anything he wants? How many schools or hospitals could that cash build? How many doctors or teachers could it train? How many children could be educated and fed and clothed and sheltered? Instead, it goes into the pockets of the charlatan with the charismatic smile telling you that you have been "saved" and have bought your way into heaven; no, don't worry about that poor hooker you murdered and dumped last week, just go to the little stall at the side and tell it to the dress-wearing creep lurking in the dark behind the mesh-covered window and he'll make you feel all better, okay? It really begs the question of why people choose to pray to an invisible power to deliver them from the trials of their lives when some simple forethought can cure most of their ills, with some simple money management to clean up the rest. Perhaps this behaviour is a throwback from the turbulent, uncertain biblical times, where anything but complete submission could get you smote from the finger of an insane deity? While there is no physical evidence of a being of immense power floating about in the sky with an itchy trigger finger, people in general are nonetheless afraid of questioning the status quo and exploring the depths of their humanity and of the universe around them, for no other reason than to hedge their bets and succumb to centuries-old bluff and superstition. We need to evolve beyond our fears if we are to understand our place in the universe, as miniscule as that appears to be.

Where was I? Oh yes, Moses collected a shit-ton of gold, silver, bronze and all manner of other goods and materials and talked people into building a tent for God and dress its occupants with the finest of cloth and resplendent with gems. Great. Speaking of gems, I feel that the stones contained in the ephod warrants closer scrutiny. You remember the ephod, yeah? The pithily-renamed BreastPiece of Decision (+2 Int, -2 Dex) referred to in Exodus 28, if my memory serves me. A particularly significant piece of priestly kit that embodied the original twelve tribes of Israel, each being represented by its own unique precious stone. Why, such a conspicuous piece of apparel would be immune to observational misinterpretations, surely? I mean, if this garment existed – and surely with the level of detail entered into in regards to it – there should be no question of its construction, yes? Well, perhaps not; Let's see what we are told in regards to this garment and its stones, shall we?

Now, the bible I'm referencing throughout my biblical travels – the New International Version or NIV – outlines the twelve stones (Ex. 39:10 – 39:13) in the breastplate in the following very specific order:

First Row

Carnelian, Chrysolite, Beryl

Second Row

Turquoise, Lapis Lazuli, Emerald

Third Row

Jacinth, Agate, Amethyst

Fourth Row

Topaz, Onyx, Jasper

Yet, if I choose to Google this magnificent breastplate of Hebrew antiquity, I find this:

First Row

Carnelian, Chrysolite, <u>Emerald</u>

Second Row

Turquoise, <u>Sapphire</u>, <u>Amethyst</u>

Third Row

Jacinth, Agate, <u>Crystal</u>

Fourth Row

<u>Beryl</u>, <u>Lapis Lazuli</u>, Jasper

Whaaat..? Seems like the stones are jumping their positions, or disappearing altogether. Where did the onyx go, and where did the sapphire grow from? Perhaps we need to look even further afield, perhaps to the James King Version (JKV) of the bible:

First Row

Sardius, Topaz, <u>Carbuncle</u>

Second Row

Emerald, Sapphire, <u>Diamond</u>

Third Row

<u>Ligure</u>, Agate, Amethyst

Fourth Row

Beryl, Onyx, Jasper

To put it in Tim "The Tool Man" Taylor's own words, "Arr-ooo..?!" Where did the diamond come from, and what the fuck is a sardius?! Sounds like a bloody fish, if you ask me. And I don't even want to speculate on a carbuncle, with a mind as alternatively-fertile as mine. How have the bibles of the world managed to screw this order of stones up so badly? It's not as if they weren't versed enough in gemcrafting that they would not know what specific gems look like, even back then, and the original stone positions (whatever they hell they were) would surely have been written down somewhere, by someone who had Moses' ear. And it's not even as if the position of the gems makes a helluva lot of difference, when you boil it down to brass tacks, so what possible benefit could there be to alter their positions? Let's try one more time, shall we? We'll spin the big bible roulette wheel and try the Common English Version (CEV); surely that will help to clear things up:

First Row

Carnelian, Topaz, Emerald Stones

Second Row

Turquoise, Sapphire, <u>Moonstone</u>

Third Row

Jacinth, Agate, Amethyst

Fourth Row

Beryl, Onyx, Jasper

Great, now we have a moonstone to contend with! I can understand – perhaps – mistaking sapphire for lapis lazuli, but only if you're half-blind, viewing the gems from a great distance and the gemcutting was complete crapola. Any person with half a brain for shiny objects, however, would easily be able to differentiate the stones. But there is still the question of why they're moving about the breastplate like a game of Chinese Checkers. Again, if how it was to be made was written down somewhere, or if the original garment existed today, then we could easily ascertain the arrangement of stones. We should also remember that, Hebrew being a right-to-left language, the stone orders could well have been described as such, instead of the instinctive left-to-right flow that we infidel English-speaking types default to when accosted with the written word. Whatever the cause, and whatever the order, I cannot see for the life of me why there should be such marked discrepancies for something which allegedly existed at some stage of our short history (and let's not get started on how many bible editions and revisions there are; over 100 at last count!).

Regardless of the above musings, it will suffice to say that all these earthly trappings were made for God at the behest of Moses (or made for Moses, at the behest of God – you make up your minds on which way it was) and then the Israelites brought all this crap to Moses, who was God-knows-where when all this was being done instead of overseeing their progress to ensure satisfaction. And, seeing that they had indeed built all his cool stuff to his satisfaction, Moses blessed them (Ex. 39:43). Personally, I would have preferred cash, but that's just the way I operate.

Finally, what biblical fiction would be complete without a little time-travelling paradox, eh..? Yeah, you know you love that stuff! And as far as paradoxes go, this one's a rip-snorter. Let me lay it down for you:

If we have a quick look at Exodus 40:17, we read, *"So the tabernacle was set up on the first day of the first month of the second year."* So far so good, right? Well, we know from the ramblings of Exodus 25-30 that a goodly amount of silver was required to make this tabernacle; silver that was collected from the refugeebrews in the census Moses conducted (under "materials used" and the sourcing of that silver, as per Exodus 38:25) and explained in Exodus 30:12 that this census was necessary so that, *"no plague will come on them when you number them."*

Now, if we skip ahead a bit to Numbers 1:1, we read something *very* interesting: *"The LORD spoke to Moses in the Tent of Meeting on the first day of the second month of the second year after the Israelites came out of Egypt. He said, 'Take a census of the whole Israelite community by their names and families, listing every man by name, one by one.'"* So, according to this, Moses received the order to conduct this census on the first day of the **second month** of the second year, one month to the day **after** the tabernacle was completed with the silver he collected from the census!

Think about that for a minute. How could Moses have been in the tabernacle, getting orders from God to conduct the census, to collect the silver needed to build the tabernacle he's already built and sitting in talking to God? If you have a logical explanation for this that does not violate the Temporal Prime Directive, do let me know, will you, readers?

Further to this: On reading a little further, when Moses made this Tent of Meeting, we are told that God descended on the tent with his cloud and filled it, such that, *"Moses could not enter the tent of meeting because the cloud had settled on it, and the glory of THE LORD filled the tabernacle"* (Ex. 40:35). Perhaps Moses should've have made the thing a little bigger to accommodate God's seven metres of height along with all the other crap inside the tent; ah well. But what sticks out like the proverbial sore thumb is that Numbers 1:1 clearly has Mose and God in the same tent, so clearly there was room for both of them, despite what Ex. 40:25 says on the matter. You see, it's things like this that really make you doubt the veracity of the bible. If you're going to pass something off as a historical fact, you should at least take the time to revise your work and make sure you're not contradicting yourself, oftentimes in the very same chapter!

Anyway, to conclude this nonsense. As a result, the Israelites stayed put when the cloud was on this tent, and only moved when the cloud lifted off it; whether it was cloud by day, or the fiery cloud by night (and how did the tent not catch fire?!) as it was referred to back on the shore of the Red Sea back in Exodus 13. And this cloud followed the hapless Israelites, apparently, throughout their travels (Ex. 40:38). And thus ends the story of Exodus.

Conclusion

"This is my simple religion. There is no need for temples; no need for complicated philosophy. Our own brain, our own heart is our temple; the philosophy is kindness." -Dalai Lama.

So, what are we to make of this, this second expedition into the twisted bowels of religion?

And Exodus was certainly a little more twisted than our previous efforts in regards to Genesis, where our narrative was relatively straight-forward. Nevertheless, we have arrived in one piece, and we need a take-away for it all to sit right in our heads. Mayhap with some garlic bread and a 1.25L coke to wash it down. Never Pepsi. I said *never*..!

Despite the bible's efforts to distract us with an endless array of measurements for tables and tabernacles, arks and courtyards and other such minutia, I have, hopefully, kept the narrative of Exodus relatively intact. Let's review the major players:

Moses: The original Basket Case, in more ways than one as it turns out. Hidden from Pharaoh's infanticidal tendencies, gets insinuated into the royal household for forty years before braining an Egyptian and fleeing. Spends another forty years hiding, breeding and getting high on burning hallucinogenic bushes, before going back to Egypt and getting all up in Ramses II's face to, "let his peeps go." Conspires with some advanced being to lure the Egyptian army into a watery grave, then spends another forty years wandering a desert with half a million people and convincing them to eat bug shit, before he consolidates his self-proclaimed divinity by carving a bunch of rules on a rock; and then he manages to defraud the Chosen People of all their gold, silver and valuables to built a tent, and installs his brother and family into the ruse, making them More Important than the rest of the Israelite rabble. Quite the scam.

God: Still as fucked up as a football bat, God's instability has not improved since our journey through Genesis. If anything, it has worsened into advanced megalomania with profound schizophrenic tendencies.

Pharaoh: Or the King of Egypt, depending on what the bible wants to call him in any given verse. Poor bastard never had a chance, really, being confronted by an uppity Hebrew before he'd managed to warm the throne with his butt heat. Made some interesting choices regarding his alleged sorcerers and never really recovered from that.

Aaron: Moses' brother, willing to go along for the ride if it meant that he got three square meals a day and all the gold he could eat.

The Elders of Israel: The 70 biggest whiners you could ever hope to meet. Would rather live in

Egyptian slavery than take a chance of freedom on the plucky newcomer. I don't really blame them, honestly.

The Chosen Peeps: 603,550 male whiners over the age of twenty, and sundry. If I were God, I would have smote (smited?) their sorry arses long ago and found myself a more evolved lot to lord it over, preferably a tribe without the inclination for deceit, bloodlust, insanity and all the other Kinder-Surprises™ we've discovered about Abe's loopy descendants back in Genesis.

The Laws of Physics: Sadly, the least-consulted and most-abused of the group. This poor guy has had a pretty rough time of it and just needs a hug.

And when it's all said and done, what do we make of this whole concept of religionism, taking just Exodus and its predecessor, Genesis, into consideration? There are certainly more holes in the plot than your average swiss cheese and dodgier morals than Hannibal Lecter, to put it mildly. And yet, if we don't believe this book to the letter, and follow its tenets without deviation, we are told that we are assigned to a fiery pit of … er, fire, to burn for all eternity, because God loves us apparently. Well, I think I can do without that kind of love, thankyou very much. And besides, if I'm dead, then I don't have a body, therefore I don't have pain receptors, therefore putting me in a lake of fire isn't going to achieve much. Unless it's some sort of spiritual lake of fire that fries spiritual energy, but who in their right mind would build a thing like that? Oh yeah, right: God created everything, didn't he, and he's not right in the head.

And then there's heaven, whatever that term might mean for you. If we're to be clinical about it, then Webster's dictionary defines heaven as, *"a place or condition of utmost happiness."* Well, okay then. But regardless of whether you define heaven as a place or a state of mind, there's also a flaw inherent in what you're going to be faced with when (or if) you find yourself there. Let's run the scenario, shall we?

So, you're in heaven. Grats to you, you freak! What is the first thing you see? Relatives? Long lost parents? Mates? Free alcohol forever? Seventy-two virgins? If there is one thing that is crystal-clear, its that everyone's idea of heaven is unique to the individual. Now, my idea of heaven (among other things) would be having Sex With Anne Hathaway Forever. This in itself presents a few problems including, but not limited to, the fact that my dearest wife, whilst being completely understanding, would still be completely nonplussed. But there's more:

Firstly, my fanciful notion of heaven might be Anne Hathaway's hell, and I can't imagine she's done anything bad enough to deserve that fate, although where there's life, there's hope..!

Secondly, although I would very much like to think that I could reunite with my parents in heaven, I also very strongly do NOT want them nearby watching me having Sex With Anne Hathaway Forever. It kinda ruins the moment, if you follow my drift, and because heaven is a "forever" kind of moment, you can imagine how that would be a problem.

Thirdly, imagine if you will some of the people you interact with on a daily basis: family, partners, workmates; all the awesome people you know from your respective peer groups, none of which deserve an eternity in hell if you had any say in the matter. Now, imagine that one workmate: such a great guy, wouldn't harm a fly, you've got nothing but respect for the man because he's so affable and easygoing, and yet working with him for any more than ten minutes makes you want to kill him in the most violent, hands-on way imaginable. Now, the guy is a saint, and undoubtedly deserves entry into heaven, but his entry soon becomes your darkest purgatory. So how to reconcile the paradox to allow each of you your respective heaven?

Thirdly, how do we reconcile the prosaic issues we're going to run into concerning our enjoying all those pleasures we denied ourselves on the material plane so we could enjoy them without guilt in heaven? It doesn't have to be Anne Hathaway; it could simply be a love of bacon, or chocolate, or some other pleasure you had hopes of making up for in your afterlife. We are bereft of our physical bodies, so what now? Conceivably, sex (or a spiritual or energy-based equivalent of it) could be possible assuming we maintain our individuality, and the pleasurable sensations we feel are a result of compatible harmonic frequencies while, heheh, "striking a chord" with Ms. Hathaway. It might be a little harder trying to eat a slice of bacon, though. I can't bring myself to imagine a line of ethereal porta-potties, let alone where the waste goes.

It would seem to me that, no matter how you look at it, we're not going to have our cake and eat it too when it comes to heaven, unless this heaven is a highly individual experience that is based solely between our ears and forever separated from anyone else's "heaven." This does mean, however, that while you may think you're meeting your relatives in heaven, it will only be in your mind (not that you will know the difference of course), and it's equally likely that a heaven involving me having Sex With Anne Hathaway Forever exists only in my mind. Which is, sadly, all it will ever be. At least you won't have your father walk in on you and give you some pointers that, "used to work for your mother," or vice versa.

More Doorknock Posers

As in my last book, please enjoy these follow-up questions for when your Sunday sleep-in is interrupted by bible-wielding bandits intent on your soul's salvation. Those silly sausages! For those of you who haven't scored my first book – and you know who you are, quit scabbing off other people already! – I shall revise the ones I put in that most esteemed volume.

Genesis

Statement: God created the universe!

Posers: If God created everything in existence, where was God prior to that? (Gen 1:1)

How could God exist where absolutely nothing existed?

If God created the Sun of the fourth day, then how did the first four days pass? (Gen. 1:14)

Statement: God created Man in his own image!

Posers: How did God arrive at the concept of Gender when there was no frame of reference, anywhere?

How was God able to create everything out of literally nothing, yet he required Adam's rib to create one more thing? (Gen. 2:21)

Why would God create so much universe for just two people to live in a garden forever?

Why would he create man with a foreskin if he was only going to get us to hack it off with a knife later anyway? (Gen. 17)

Statement: The Apple and the Expulsion.

Posers: Where would Adam and Eve have found a needle and thread in the Garden of Eden to sew fig leaves together? (Gen. 3:8)

Why would God make clothes for Adam and Eve, then turf them out? If they're going to be punished for eternity, then whether or not he gave them clothing would be irrelevant. (Gen. 3:21)

Statement: Cain and Abel.

Posers: How did Cain, with 360° of direction to choose from, manage to find the land of Nod first time? (Gen. 4:16)

Why was it called Nod, and who decided to call it that? (Gen. 4:18)

If it was already there when Cain went off, then who was populating Nod? There was only supposed to be four people on the planet at this stage of the game (well, three now, thanks to Cain's impulsive misuse of a rock).

Who was Cain afraid was going to kill him, earning him a Mark of Cain from God to protect him? Protect him from whom?

What was Cain's wife's name?

Where did she come from?

Statement: Noah and the ark (any reference).

Posers: So was it *two* of every animal, or *sixteen*?

How do you even go from *"male and female each of their kind"* to *"seven pairs of clean animals and one pair of unclean animals"* without raising some serious questions? (Gen. 7:2 – 7:3)

Why would God even bother with saving the unclean animals when he's cleansing the earth of sin anyway? Isn't "unclean" a sin?

How did God save two of every fish and drown the rest of them?

How did Noah open the doors on the ark from the *inside,* when God himself shut them inside the ark from the *outside*? (Gen. 7:16)

Why would Noah save all the animals, only to kill them with fire as soon as he left the ark? No, the clean ones were burned as well. (Gen. 8:20)

Why would God be happy with Noah burning the animals after all the effort expended to save them? Is he mental?

How do you account for the appearance and disappearance of 4.5 trillion gigalitres of water?

Statement: Noah found naked, curses Canaan.

Posers: What the fuck did Canaan do? It was Ham who found his naked drunky father, and yet Noah curses Ham's innocent son? What an arsehole! (Gen. 9:24)

Statement: The Covenant of Circumcision

Posers: What sort of God justifies an act of self-mutilation? Isn't your body a temple to God?

If Man was created perfectly by a perfect God, then why do humans even have a foreskin?

What's the deal with the Abram/Abraham name change? (Gen. 17:5)

How does God changing Sarai's name to Sarah affect her fertility in any significant way?

Statement: Onanism and its implications

Posers: This story/fable is about birth control and thwarting God's orders; it was never about self-pleasure (Gen. 38:9).

Onan was having sex with his dead brother's wife, not masturbating. Get your story right.

Statement: Joseph and his Silver Cup

Posers: How did the Captain of the Royal Guard identify the exact silver cup *before* he began searching Joseph's brothers for it? (Gen. 44:6)

If Joseph's cup gave him powers of divination, would he not have seen the theft in advance and taken steps to prevent that?

If Joseph planted this cup deliberately, then surely you agree that it's not a very good moral lesson to impart, framing people for theft like that with no appropriate consequences?

Exodus

Statement: The birth of Moses

Posers: When, exactly, was Moses born? Only one date matches to when his adopted brother Ramesses II was alive, and Moses was already 88 when he was born (and eight years into his 40-year desert trek); how does *that* work?

Moses' brother Aaron was only 3 years older than Moses, so how did he dodge being killed by Pharaoh's baby killing squad?

It was a pretty sweet swindle, getting Pharaoh's daughter to pay for Moses' own mother to wet-nurse him!

Statement: Moses' burning bush

Posers: The bush Moses saw burning is known for producing hallucinogenic smoke, so it's no wonder he was seeing faces in the flames.

Statement: Moses' return to Egypt

Posers: Why the fuck would God choose Moses to be his champion, only to try killing him on the way back to Egypt? (Ex. 4:24)

Are foreskins God's kryptonite? It seemed to work pretty well for Moses' wife when she wiped it on Moses' foot that one time..?

Statement: Moses and the Plagues

Posers: You realize that Moses was 117 years old when Ramesses II ascended to the throne of Egypt, yes?

If Moses turned, "all of the water" to blood as claimed, then how did the Pharaoh's sorcerers replicate that feat? (Ex. 7:19)

If the sorcerers turned the blood back into water in order to replicate this plague, why didn't they just *leave it as water*, nullifying the plague altogther?

If *all* of Egypt's water was turned into blood, how come the Egyptian people were able to dig down alongside the Nile to access fresh water?

If the frog plague "vanished" the next day, how come the Egyptians were putting frog corpses onto piles later in the chapter? (Ex. 8:13)

During the plague of darkness, it is claimed that, "<u>noone could see anyone else</u> *or move about for three days, but the Israelites had light*". How was this observed if nothing could be seen? (Ex. 10:22)

How did Pharaoh's officers (on his command) bring Moses to the palace if they couldn't see anyone else? How would they have found him?

Pharaoh screams, "Get out of my sight!" at Moses during the plague of darkness. How was Pharaoh able to see Moses in total darkness?

Statement: The Passover

Posers: What's God's problem with yeast?

Is God gluten-intolerant?

Do you really think killing someone is an acceptable punishment for finding yeast in their home during Passover? (Ex.

Did you know that Dogon people of Mali consider the front door of their house to be representing the owner's genitals? Do you feel there's a suspicious parallel there between that and the blood on the doorframe representing the Covenant of Circumcision, and perhaps a usurping of the Dogon culture to some extent?

Statement: The Exodus Proper

Posers: Assuming that other gods exist, why would God say not to worship other gods? Isn't God the only god? Did God create other gods? If so, why would he divvy up his powers?

If there were other gods in Egypt, why didn't they group up and eliminate this crazy Hebrew god?

What velocity of wind would God have needed to provide to part the Red Sea, given it was a trench nine miles long and two hundred metres deep?

How would a fragile, squishy human body possibly survive such a wind velocity without being spat out the other end like a spitball and rag-dolling the length of Saudi Arabia?

Statement: 40 years of wandering the desert

Posers: Did you know that the "manna from heaven" God provided to the Israelites was Honeydew, which is in fact an insect excretion?

Why would God give the Israelites bug shit to eat? Did they not bring their own flocks and herds with them when they fled Egypt?

Statement: Mount Sinai and The Tablets

Posers: Why would God create the Ten Commandments, and then add a whole bunch of provisos, addendums and quid-pro-quos?

Why does God's commandments for the preparation of his descending to earth sound suspiciously like a Radiation Containment Protocol?

Why does God need Moses to make all these tables and tabernacles and lampstands and so on? Can't God just Create it like he did before with literally everything (except Eve)?

God specifically asked Moses to make the ark, table, tabernacle and so on to extremely precise specifications. Why did Moses subcontract this task? Isn't that cheating?

Statement: The Tabernacle and Et cetera.

Posers: Exodus 40:17 states that the tabernacle was erected on the first day of the first month of the second year.

Silver was needed for the tabernacle. This silver was given by voluntary offerings from the refugeebrews (Exodus 38:25). This numbering was explained in Exodus 30:12.

Now, Numbers 1:1 says that on the first of the *second month of the second year*, Moses was ordered to take the census.

Therefore, the amount of the silver could not have been known in the first month of the second year. So how could the tabernacle have been erected in the *first* month of the second year already, before the census was even ordered on the *second* month of that year?

Statement: Moses and the Glory of God

Posers: How is it possible for Moses to speak to God, *"face to face, as one speaks to a friend"* in Ex. 33:11, and then reconcile that with Ex. 33:20, *"for no one may see me and live"*? You can't have it both ways, so pick a struggle.

Why was it okay for years for God to rap with Abram, Isaac, Jacob, Joseph and Moses, but now suddenly it's a death sentence? Did God suddenly get acne or something?

For God to have covered the cleft in the rock containing Moses with his hand, God would have had to have been about seven metres tall if we were created in his image. Do you think this explains the Nephilim to some degree, in that God and his winged cronies were sexually assaulting humans at the Dawn of Creation?

Why are there such profound discrepancies regarding the position of the twelve precious stones on the Breast Plate of Decision (+2 Int, -2 Dex), and just as many discrepancies regarding the actual stones used in the piece? Surely such an important religious relic would not attract so many differing views about its construction?

Last-Ditch Desperate Statement: Oh, but that's all the Old Testament; we only believe in the New Testament!

Posers: If the bible is the literal Word of God, then you can't just pick an choose which bits you believe and which bits you don't; you either have to believe ALL of it, or none of it.

The bible is approximately 75% Old Testament and 25% New Testament. You can't just dismiss three quarters of the Book of God because it doesn't suit you.

If that lot doesn't send your uninvited Sunday caller running for the gate, then nothing will. You're welcome..!

Final Thoughts

So, to my final thoughts on Exodus and the bible in general, now having covered two of its books, Genesis and Exodus:

It is still my considered opinion that we are either dealing with a complete fiction or, if there *are* elements of truth to these events, that they were heavily weighted toward being some extraterrestrial event that was misinterpreted by minds too simple to understand advanced technology;

It is my hope that I have entertained as much as I have enlightened you in your journey through my second book. Again, if you have read this book, and have enjoyed it, I hope you will do it (and me!) a favour and recommend it to your like-minded friends and associates. Word of mouth is the most powerful recommendation a book can get, above any other pithy advertising mechanism, so my book's fate is truly in your hands! As per my previous book, it is available online and on demand from your favourite book repository;

Once again, the interpretations contained therein are mine, and mine alone. You may or may not agree with the interpretations, but that is your choice as a discerning reader. When you consider that the bible has changed so much in the way of alterations, redactions, revisions and reinterpretations, my humble offering is merely one in a cast of thousands. Either you'll love it or you'll hate it; please arrange yourselves accordingly;

While I've had a lot of fun dissecting Exodus here today, and Genesis before that, I have been asked by numerous people to, "do the Quran," or to, "do the New Testament," but there are a couple of fairly good reasons why I won't;

a. I don't want to have a Fatma out against me;

b. I'd only be repeating what I've said in my first two evaluations.

It is my fervent hope that, by introducing a few new possibilities and highlighting the need to be objective and rational with any claim or assertion, you can use your newly-forged skills and improve your ability to spot a con job when you see it. This doesn't have to apply solely to religion; it could be the guy down the road with the 3-card monte table, or a corrupt politician angling for your vote, or even the "love of your life" that you've found after winning that $180 million the day before (don't forget me in your will, okay?). Being more aware of what's being asked and running the logic through your head, will not only save you grief in the short term; it can also help you spot and avoid future pitfalls on your own personal paths to success;

Remember that, when you boil it all down, no one knows what will happen to us after death, at least until we get there and we find out for ourselves. Until that happens, it is incumbent on us all to be the nicest people we can possibly be to each other, and let the dice fall where they may. I don't think any god will condemn you to hell for being a good and kind person. And if these "gods" just happen to be UNreasonable..? Then I guess we're screwed either way, aren't we, so we might as well just be nice to people anyway, and ignore the stupid rules about not owning a red car. It makes Life easier for us all.

And that's Exodus! Thanks for reading, and stay logical!

Online References

As well as the online version of the New International Version (NIV) of the bible, the following sources were referenced to either verify or refute some of the more outrageous claims contained that so-called Book of Truth. Feel free to verify these sources for yourself in your own time, which were correct at the time of writing this; I'm too busy engaging in all manner of debauchery to assist you effectively, so enjoy, and just let yourselves out when you're done.

Desert of Sin drinking water:

https://www.iflscience.com/environment/simple-tree-branch-filter-makes-dirty-water-drinkable/

Weight of Bronze:

Http://www.columbiametals.com/technical/weight-calculator

The Tabernacle Paradox:

https://hermeneutics.stackexchange.com/questions/31774/how-can-the-tabernacle-have-been-erected-in-the-second-year

Correlation between hand length and human height:
https://www.biomedscidirect.com/878/study_of_correlation_between_human_height_and_h

and_length_in_residents_of_mumbai/articlesca tegories

Dogon People and their Architecture:

https://books.google.com.au/books?id=IXmsz KFQ7MUC&pg=PA34&lpg=PA34&dq=the+do or+of+the+house+in+bodily+reference&source =bl&ots=PabTMWUcS3&sig=MWfxcaPgn9boa qBZm3KipHagghc&hl=en&sa=X&ved=0ahUK Ewi0ht-o6PzbAhUFipQKHcjJDpkQ6AEIPTAH#v=one page&q=the%20door%20of%20the%20house%2 0in%20bodily%20reference&f=false

Frankincense and Myrrh, uses and values:

https://www.history.com/news/a-wise-mans-cure-frankincense-and-myrrh

Girding one's Loins:

https://lp.israelbiblicalstudies.com/lp_iibs_bib lical_hebrew_gird_loins_new-en.html?cid=47970&adgroupid=-1&utm_source=Community&utm_medium=FB _insights&utm_campaign=BIB_EN_COM_FB_ Gird_Loins_2017-11-01_47970

Quail traits and behaviours:

https://wildbirdsonline.com/blogs/news/qua il-behavior-traits-and-characteristics

Ramesses II:

https://en.wikipedia.org/wiki/Ramesses_II

Moses, historical references:

https://en.wikipedia.org/wiki/Moses

Couinaud Classification of Hepatic Segments:

https://radiopaedia.org/articles/couinaud-
classification-of-hepatic-segments

Capacitance Calculator for rectangular boxes:

https://chemandy.com/calculators/rectangula
r-capacitor-calculator.htm

http://www.energeticforum.com/renewable-
energy/4940-ark-covenant-replications-study-
2.html